HOPE *for the* Hopeless

Freedom from Anxiety and Depression Is Possible

Lyn STAFFORD

LISE Publishing
Box 2198
St. Marys, Ontario, Canada, N4X 1A1

HOPE FOR THE HOPELESS
Freedom From Anxiety and Depression Is Possible

Copyright©2019 by Lyn Stafford

All rights reserved. This book is protected by copyright laws. No part of it may be copied or reproduced or transmitted by any means without the written permission of the author.

This book contains the opinions and ideas of the author and in no way should it be regarded as a substitute for professional medical treatment.
Some names have been changed to protect privacy.

Edited by Shirley Lise and Felicia Trickey
Cover Photo by Jessica Thiessen

ISBN: 9781090227836

Imprint: Independently published

Manufactured
in the United States of America

*This book is dedicated to all
those who have suffered with a mood
disorder of any type, to those who have a loved
one living with this battle, and to the ones who
have had to live through the unthinkable--
the death of a loved one due
to these disorders.*

Contents

Introduction	5
1 THE POWER OF THE PAST	7
2 SETTING THE STAGE	12
3 THE BEGINNINGS OF A BREAKDOWN	20
4 OUT OF CONTROL	29
5 SEEKING HELP	36
6 ANOTHER BREAKDOWN	46
7 HOSPITALIZED	59
8 THE WORST WAR OF MY LIFE	67
9 HOPE AGAIN!	74
10 HELP TO THE RESCUE	81
11 THE ROCKY ROAD TO RECOVERY	87
12 NEW REVELATION	95
13 ADDRESSING THE BODY	99
14 SOUL AND SPIRIT HEALTH	110
15 DETOXIFICATION	119
16 FINAL THOUGHTS	125
Acknowledgements	134
Resources	138

Introduction

When someone suggested I write a book, it seemed impossible, as English was always my weakest subject. I could never write like the A students, with allegories and fancy words that flowed together. But here I am today, writing in my own way because I feel I have something important to say, something that could save a life, or help someone know, how to save a life.

After being diagnosed with a major depressive disorder in my early twenties, I didn't think I would ever live a normal, happy life again. I thought life would always be a battle and that my racing thoughts would never stop. I assumed I would always require anti-anxiety medications and high doses of antidepressants to stay sane.

I thought I would always feel alone, trapped in my own head, but today this is not the case.

I can say my life today is filled with more joy than I ever had. I am able to live a full life, even volunteer in a psychiatric hospital, which as you read this book, you will see is a miracle. There were many things that contributed to the health I have today which I feel could apply to anyone struggling mentally and emotionally. I don't claim to have all the answers, but through my journey, I have discovered that staying well is possible, with work and a willingness to go through the process. There is no one silver bullet that will cure all, but rather many areas that need to be addressed when breaking free from depression and anxiety.

I believe that we consist of three parts, the body, soul, and spirit. I see the body as the physical part of us, the soul as our mind, will and emotions and our spirit as the part that can connect to a higher power, along with containing our sense of identity, creativity, and conscience. Healing will be limited if we do not address all three areas. It is extremely important that these three areas be looked at when treating mood disorders such as depression and anxiety.

I am a living example of how darkness can turn to light, how someone can find relief from pain, how sickness can change to health and death can turn into life!

I have been in the place where death seemed like a better option because the pain was so great and nothing was taking it away. However, I can say with confidence that there is hope for those who are living in the dark night of the soul, right now.

When I wasn't well, it seemed easier for me to focus on the worst-case scenarios. I seemed to notice anyone around me with depression and anxiety who were not improving far more than anyone who had healed from it. Every day I dwelled on the medications that didn't work for others and the negative side effects that seemed to make people worse especially during my stay in the psychiatric hospital. It took all my willpower to notice anyone getting better or staying better and I truly felt beyond hope. Even if I did hear about someone recovering, I still felt that my case was too severe to ever have improvement.

Well, I'm writing today, completely recovered, to share a best-case scenario, for anyone who needs to hear it. There is always hope for the hopeless and I pray that you will believe and feel it as you read this book!

Chapter 1

THE POWER OF THE PAST

Wednesday, October 17, 2012, is a day I will never forget and never want to repeat. It was on this day that I found myself standing in a hospital room of the psychiatric ward in Kingston General Hospital with tears pouring down my face, full of anxiety, and wondering how on Earth I was going to survive. How did a person like me end up in a place like this? The psychiatric ward had been one of my worst fears for most of my life, and here I was facing it head-on, whether I wanted to or not. If someone had told me years ago I would end up in here, I would have never believed them, as I always thought I was a strong person, a fighter, someone who could handle anything. Besides this, I was an extrovert with a bubbly personality who loved to have fun, had many friends, and most of all was a person who was very dedicated to my Christian faith, serving God where I could. I also tried to be a good wife and mother to my two children. This hospital I was in was for others, people who were weak, needy, less spiritual, and quieter, or so I thought. Boy, I was SO wrong!

My first introduction to any kind of mental illness goes back to when I was quite young. My grandmother had been diagnosed with paranoid schizophrenia and my uncle also struggled with a mental health condition. I didn't have much of a relationship with either one of them because of this. I don't have any memories of spending time with my uncle and as for my grandmother, I have just two clear memories of her and they weren't exactly warm and fuzzy. The first memory is of a visit she had with us where we sat down for a meal. Once we started to eat, I heard her say to my mom, "Shirley, your bread is full of mold." My mom then replied by telling her that the bread was fresh and there was no mold on it, but grandma insisted that there was even after being told a number of times there wasn't. She then deemed it unsafe and would not eat it because, in her mind, it was bad. The second memory I have of her is during another visit where I heard her telling my mom that there were snakes all over the house. I was about five years old at the time, so I didn't understand at all why she was talking this way when it was clear that there were no snakes in the house.

I don't remember any other conversations we had with her in our home, but I do remember one day after a visit, grandma left without saying goodbye to me. I thought it was odd and wondered why so asked my mom about it. She explained to me that she had asked her to leave before she had a chance to say bye because grandma was sick and needed to go back to the hospital right away. We didn't talk about grandma's sickness much, but I came to understand that she was "sick in her head" and needed to live in a hospital because of it.

At age fifty-seven, my grandma passed away from a brain aneurysm which was very sad for all of us, especially considering how it happened. She had been experiencing a horrible headache while being out for a walk one day when she collapsed on the street. The police were called to come pick her up. When they arrived at the scene, they assumed she was drunk because of the way she looked, as she would have appeared very unattractive due to the lack of personal hygienic care resulting from her mental illness. They decided to drop her off at her sister-in law's home so she could sleep it off. Fortunately, her sister-in-law knew that she was not a drinker and that she indeed was not well. She called an ambulance to come and take grandma to the hospital so she could get proper care and figure out what was really going on. When grandma arrived, however, the hospital staff was not much help. They took the same position as the police had taken regarding the seriousness of her condition based on her appearance and left her unattended in the waiting room for several hours before looking at her. When it was finally clear to hospital staff that my grandmother was extremely sick and that she needed immediate care, it was too late. She was transported to another hospital and put in the ICU, but by that time she was nonresponsive and put on life-support as she could not breathe on her own. She was then considered brain dead and passed away a few days later in the hospital when life support was removed.

Here was an example of someone with a mental health condition wrongly judged on appearance and viewed with disdain by those in a position to help, assuming they were dealing with a case of substance abuse instead of looking into the real issue. It makes me sad to think that this could have been avoided, that the turn out could have been very different if the police would have paid attention to the needs of my grandmother and not judged her by her looks. Even though mental health is discussed a lot more openly today, there are still many instances where people are judged by the way they look because of their mental state and die an early death resulting from undiagnosed and untreated health problems.

When I attended my grandmas funeral, I remember feeling sick to my stomach as I looked at her laying in the coffin, wondering if I would end up with a mental illness like her someday.

My uncle, who was my grandma's son, also spent a lot of his life struggling with mental health issues so psychiatric hospitals were a normal part of his life as well. Because of street drug use, his function was further impaired, resulting in jail time and spending his life in group homes until he passed away. Hearing stories of traumatic episodes in his life only amplified the growing fear I already had. I don't remember visiting him much at all, but the times I did see him, it put an extreme scare into me of him and anyone else who slightly resembled him. This is probably what really started me stigmatizing mental illness in my mind, thinking that anyone who had it looked rough, was unkempt, smelled unpleasant, was dysfunctional, and had nothing to offer anyone. I'm ashamed to even say it, but this is what I believed at the time. This was back in the 1970s when mental health was viewed as completely different than it is today. No one seemed to talk about it for one thing, which I believe caused a lot of needless suffering, shame, stigma placing, embarrassment, and most of all fear.

There is a verse in the Christian bible that I love which talks about how "the truth sets us free." Fear of mentally ill people and becoming that way myself had a huge grip on my life until one day the truth set me free and it happened in a way I would never have expected. I would learn that mental illness does not have a certain look, but can happen to anyone, rich, poor, beautiful, unattractive, people who exude an unpleasant aroma, people who don't, the old, the young, those raised in a good home, and those who aren't.

Chapter 2

SETTING THE STAGE

I was born to Luke and Shirley Lise in 1974 and raised in a small Dutch community with a population of about 2,500 including animal pets. Life became busy, loud, chaotic, and challenging at times as three brothers were born after me. Eight years would go by before I would finally be given my first sister. I was so excited when she was born that I could hardly control myself. I loved to take care of her, read to her, play with her, and even change her diaper even though it was a cloth one! Another brother and sister followed shortly after to complete our family of nine.

It seemed to be quite normal in the Dutch community to have many children. Most of my friends back then came from families of six siblings or more. One of my closest friends had parents who fostered and adopted children while also having five biological children. They often had ten children living in the house at once, so when both of our families got together, it was quite the sight and sound. My friend and I jokingly had a little phrase we loved to say when we answered the phone. Her last name was Jefferson and mine was Lise at the time, so when the phone rang, I would answer, "Hello, Lise Safari, can I help you?" and when she was called, she would answer, "Hello, Jefferson Jungle, can I help you?" Even though there seemed to be kids everywhere I went, I enjoyed life, at least most of the time.

My dad also came from a big family. He was the third youngest of ten children. His family immigrated to Canada from Holland when he was three years old and settled into the small town of Drayton, Ontario. We attended the Dutch Christian Reformed Church in the mornings and evenings on Sundays and at least once during the week. We had soup with meatballs in it every Sunday for lunch which was tradition, as well as was "Olie bollen" (which is similar to a small apple fritter sprinkled with icing sugar), on New Year's Eve. We ate croquettes at the yearly bazaar and sucked on KING or FAAM peppermints during the church services. My mom didn't like to feed us sugar balls, so we didn't get the peppermints from her, but still always managed to get them from somewhere along with my favorite, salted "droppies!" Droppies are similar to black licorice with extra salt and shaped like a thick nickel. Any Dutchie will know about this sweet yet salty treat!

There were many things I enjoyed about my life, but there were also many times I was struggling, especially emotionally. Talking about my emotions to anyone was foreign. No one seemed to talk about "things they were going through," or "how they were feeling." Along with suppressed emotion, there was a harshness in the Dutch community where physical and verbal abuse seemed to be the norm. I later learned that this harshness was often caused by the experiences the Dutch had during the World Wars. Because of all the trauma of war these people had seen and experienced, they were accustomed to just trying to survive and not dealing with the emotional impact at all because it was the only way they could cope.

Counseling sessions were not attended, at least not in our circles, so those struggling did not receive the healing they needed from their past. This led to most of them developing an inability to recognize not only their own emotional needs but the emotional needs of others.

The elementary school I attended was made up mostly of Dutch families and staff members. It was a place where abuse took place even though it was a Christian School. I remember being in grade six and walking down the hall with a jar of paint when I accidentally dropped it. A teacher came up to me and demanded in an extremely harsh tone that I clean the mess right away. I went to get some paper towels to clean it up and began to wipe up the paint. When he saw this, he started to yell at me "You think we can afford you wasting new paper towels? Definitely not! Now empty one of the garbage cans and use the used ones in there!" I was taken back at first but seemed to recover quickly as I was quite used to his emotional outbursts and abuse.

Many times he would whack students with a skate guard across the rear or slap his yardstick down hard on our desks an inch away from our fingers as a scare tactic. One day when it was my turn to receive the skate guard on my behind, I decided to shove a bunch of hard textbooks down my backside to try and soften the blow. I thought it was funny but unfortunately, the teacher did not and I probably received a harder blow than was intended after emptying out the books.

The other teachers were similar in that one of them had disciplined a grade three student by tying him to his desk with a rope! The rope was put around his arms and body so that while the student cried, there was nothing he could do to wipe his dripping nose except sit there in total humiliation. There were many times we would be yelled at, grabbed, or verbally abused.

My parents loved me and my siblings and did their best, but because they were raised in harsh environments themselves and abuse was what they too experienced as a way of discipline, they did not advocate for us. My dad was raised very strictly in the Dutch community with physical and emotional abuse being the norm, and although my mom had no Dutch background, she had her own childhood of trauma and dysfunction. When she married my dad, she adapted quite quickly to his culture. Together their discipline methods were often harsh which caused a lot of bitterness and anger in us as children. Not only were discipline measures harsh, but they were not necessarily balanced out with gentleness and kindness which may have helped to diffuse the anger. There was no discussing the offenses that we as children committed, as the saying "children should be seen and not heard" was the reality. This in itself was traumatic for me even though I didn't realize it at the time, as all these emotions were being stuffed down over and over again, waiting to explode.

Many people in the Dutch culture suffered the same way that I did and the repercussions on the mind and body were often tragic. Many people suffered and still suffer from emotional and physical ailments because of the mental stress on their minds. It has been proven many times over that emotional stress and woundedness can deeply affect the physical body along with the spirit.

Because abuse was so normal in most of the Dutch community, it is understandable that emotions just ended up repressed and after awhile immunity kicked in and a "thick skin," so to speak, developed. I know for myself, I unknowingly carried the belief that emotions such as sadness, anxiety, grief, discouragement, and the like, were not important or worth talking about and that laughter and joking around could get rid of them all. I have memories of going to places and seeing other kids expressing emotion that I felt were negative like sadness or anger and thinking how needy they looked. This repulsed me and I was certain I didn't want to look or act like them, so laughter became my best friend. I loved to have fun and would do anything to have it even if it meant being a brat in school.

It seemed like so much fun to do what I wasn't supposed to be doing and I clued in early that I was able to receive the attention that I didn't always get at home. Sometimes that meant going out the window in the middle of class just to see if I could get away with it or talking and laughing out loud so I would be asked to leave the class. I especially enjoyed doing this in high school as it meant I could spend my time at a close- by donut shop instead of at a desk. I was happy to have a few other Dutch friends who were just as eager to involve themselves in the action with me. Often there would be 3 or 4 of us going to the donut shop together at least once a week which made my fun even more fun!

Life to me was all about having fun and laughing hysterically, and my friends and I were somehow able to make a joke about everything and anything, even the abusive situations. It was not that I never experienced anything other than laughter and joy, but that I rarely ever talked about or expressed anything else. If I did, I would hide it especially when I felt I was going to cry. I would hide in public washrooms, cars or my bedroom when I felt I couldn't control the tears for fear of anyone seeing me in this state. I did not want to give people the impression that I was weak or needy as it was embarrassing to me.

Unfortunately, there were many more traumatic events that took place in my younger years that would add to the heap of unresolved emotions.

There was one incident, in particular, that was quite traumatic and took place when I was only three years old. My parents, my brother and I were living in a rented cottage near a lake at the time. I had been playing with a five-year-old boy down near the lake one day. Bobbys' parents often allowed him to go down unsupervised because he knew the rules which included staying away from the water. My mom allowed me to go with him one day, trusting that he would make sure I also stayed away from the water. However, Bobby somehow ended up in the water that day and right before my eyes, I watched him drown without even knowing it. I must have sensed something wasn't right though as I quickly ran to the cottage to tell my mom that a fish was eating Bobby. My mother knew immediately that something was terribly wrong and came running down to a gruesome and horrifying sight. Bobby had been under the water for twenty minutes and had already passed away when my mom pulled his lifeless body from the water onto the dock. I was told that the scene after was horrific as Bobby's parents found out the news and began to react hysterically. Even though I don't remember the incident or aftermath, I am sure it impacted every part of me and played a role in my future mental health and wellness.

Other traumas that happened to me at a young age were when close family members became chronically ill and I was brought along to visit them close to their deaths. Two of my young uncles were diagnosed with cancers in their early twenties and in horrible pain before their deaths. I would go along to the hospital with my parents to visit, but feel sick to my stomach, full of anxiety as all the tubes and noises would terrify me, along with seeing the bruises and bumps on their bodies.

Other close relatives passed away from different illnesses but watching them decline during our hospital visits and then seeing them in their coffins put great anxiety and fear into me.

There were many more experiences that I felt traumatized from early on in my life. The ones that affected me the most include being seriously bitten by a dog, witnessing five choking incidents with my siblings, seeing a number of serious accidents, being in car accidents, being in a tornado and almost drowning. Each one of these experiences caused me great stress and fear and now that I know so much more about the effects of trauma, I can say that they definitely impacted my being in a negative way. They weren't processed properly at all either which made things worse. The only way I processed them was by trying to get rid of the memories of them the only way I knew how- by pretending they didn't affect me and didn't exist.

Being the oldest of seven children put me in a position where I was often in charge of taking care of others. This in itself is not a bad thing, but with me, I often felt responsible for my siblings even when I wasn't babysitting them. I'm sure this is quite normal for the oldest child in a family, and although not necessarily bad, it became a habit that I developed with everyone. I felt responsible for people all the time even though I didn't realize it. I felt responsible for their happiness, their peace, their health, their safety, their faith, and their general well being which eventually proved to be detrimental to me. There were other factors that were also setting me up for major mental challenges in the future. One is that I cared way too much what people thought and would do anything and everything to keep the peace. I had friends in my life who would use me over and over again because I allowed them to by not speaking up when I disagreed with something. This caused great anger inside me, yet I would not acknowledge it. I felt like a volcano ready to explode at times, but I would somehow manage to shove the burning fire down and smile or laugh with my friends as though all was well.

In the last few years, I have learned about the four personalities: sanguine, melancholy, choleric, and phlegmatic. I recommend everyone do some type of personality quiz because it is extremely helpful in understanding how you are wired to process events and how others with different personalities process these same events. Even though we have traits from all personality types, there is usually one that is dominant. When I did the quiz online, it was very obvious that I was a strong sanguine. Sanguine personalities can feel extreme emotions but have an ability to move on from them quite quickly. If the emotion is anger or sadness, a typical sanguine will feel the emotion but then be able to switch into "happy" mode quite quickly. This can be a very good thing but only if the emotions are processed and dealt with properly before moving on. Because I did not do this, many of my emotions were just being shoved down more and more, waiting to be released someday in a way that I could never have imagined. Of course, as a child and teen, I had no idea that I had been repressing anything and that doing so could affect me in a negative way. I certainly didn't have any idea that it could actually encourage a mental illness, especially for someone who was genetically predisposed to it. In time, I would find out the hard way that it can.

Chapter 3

THE BEGINNINGS OF A BREAKDOWN

I moved out for the first time at the age of 17 to go live with a friend of mine and her family. They only lived about 20 minutes from my parents so I could go visit if I liked but could have the space I seemed to need as well.

I attended my friends' high school and while I mostly only had an interest in playing sports there, I managed to complete grade 12 before going on to hairstyling school the following September.

I loved almost everything about hairstyling school! My best friend came with me for one thing and many of the other girls taking the course were a lot of fun to learn with. Besides learning how to cut and style hair, I also loved talking with the customers that would come in to see us. At first, I was extremely nervous about it but after time, I became quite confident in striking up conversations and figuring out what clients wanted. The students and I also shared a lot of good laughs especially about all the mistakes we made that year. My biggest mistakes happened with my first client – an older man probably in his fifties. I was the first one in my class to perform a haircut on a real person instead of a mannequin so when I was asked to do the cut, many students were peeking around the corner watching me. I was a nervous wreck but pretended I knew exactly what I was doing. That didn't last long though because as I began to cut around the mans' right ear, I nicked it with the blade of the scissors. I didn't nick it a lot but it doesn't take much to have an ear bleed ferociously from a tiny cut with hair cutting scissors. As the blood began dripping down his shoulder, I froze in terror. The teacher came running to try and stop the bleeding. She put some hydrogen peroxide on the wound and then put a nice big fluffy piece of cotton on his ear to help absorb any of the bleeding. I can't remember how many times I apologized before somehow getting the courage to keep cutting his hair. The man was very gracious, thank goodness! But just when I thought it couldn't get any worse I went and nicked his left ear. Once again blood began to gush out! I was absolutely mortified and wanted to quit hairstyling school right there and then! The teacher came running again to do the same procedure she did for the right ear and topped it off with another lovely piece of cotton. The man now looked like he had earmuffs on! I seriously thought my career was over already and I hadn't even started it yet. I'm guessing that it was extremely humiliating for this poor man but I know it was for me. Again I apologized over and over and thankfully I was able to laugh about it with him and make a few jokes to which he was once again very gracious and understanding. After this, my teacher suggested that I move ears when I'm trying to cut around them which I hadn't done because it wasn't possible on the plastic heads we practiced on. It was a very good lesson to learn.

 After graduating from hairstyling school, I worked at a camp in Brantford, Ontario called Circle Square Ranch. A close friend of mine had asked me for years to work there with her in the summers but I had never taken a summer off to do it. I graduated from the school in June and didn't have any immediate plans so it seemed like the perfect summer to go work on a ranch. This is exactly what I did and I thoroughly enjoyed myself. During this summer I met a new friend who I became quite close with. She ended up asking me to go to Kingston, Ontario at the end of the summer to help her move into her apartment as she was attending Queens University. I decided to go along with her and her parents to help her move in. Kingston was about a 3.5-hour drive from the ranch so we ended up staying there for a couple of days. In the car on the drive there, my friend and I began to discuss the idea of me looking for a job in Kingston so we could live in the same city. I loved the idea as most of my other friends had moved away to different colleges and universities anyways. I also loved adventure and living in a city seemed very exciting and adventurous to me.

Soon after we arrived in Kingston, there happened to be a newspaper on the table in the kitchen of my friend's new apartment. I picked it up and began to read the job listings in the Classifieds section. I very quickly saw an ad for a salon that was hiring a junior hairstylist which was perfect because that's exactly what I was. My friend and I got so excited that we started planning every detail of my life in Kingston before I even went for an interview. As I dialed the number for the job I remember being extremely nervous at the idea of it not working out so I decided to say a quick prayer when I was done on the phone begging God to let this work out.

The person on the end of the phone invited me for an interview the next day which really excited me. She had asked me to bring in a model which needed to be a person who would allow me to cut their hair in front of the owner so they could see how I cut and styled hair.

The problem was I didn't know anyone in Kingston except my friend and she just had her hair cut by her sister recently. So, we decided to ask her one roommate if she needed a cut. The amazing thing is that this roommate had booked herself a hair appointment earlier in the week but ended up canceling it for one reason or another. She happily agreed to be my model which was wonderful. We still giggle to this day thinking about how I dug the comb into her neck when I was combing her hair because I was so nervous during the interview.

I ended up getting the job that day and I couldn't have been happier. I moved to Kingston within a few days and have made it a home ever since.

Soon after starting my new job I met a man named Jeff Stafford at a local church. We were part of the young adult's group there. He seemed to take quite an interest in me and I found out later that he was looking for a woman to date who looked good in a ball cap, had nice legs and straight teeth. Apparently, I met the criteria. Thankfully he met my criteria as well so we began to date a few months later at the age of 20 and were married two years later on April 26, 1997.

During our first year of marriage, we both found ourselves quite busy between work and friends. I worked almost full-time hours in the hair salon and then did the hair of my friends on the side at home which I thoroughly enjoyed. Jeff was working at a headhunting placement in Ottawa a couple days a week in hope that it would give him some good experience for the future. We both played sports, were part of a thriving church, had many friends, and loved married life.

It was one year after we got married that Jeff was offered what we thought sounded like an amazing opportunity in Toronto, Ontario. He was hired by a big company to work as a headhunter there. We didn't think twice about it but started looking for an apartment right away as the job was starting in less than a week. Looking back it seems so irrational that we did not really even think about what we were leaving behind nor pray about our decision, as we had often prayed about much smaller decisions. I guess we were just way too excited about him getting a job in his field to care.

In less than a week we had packed up our belongings, said goodbye to our friends, quit any sports we were involved in, I quit my job, and we waited for our UHAUL to haul us away. Unfortunately, we had no idea that endless problems lay ahead and that fighting off constant stressors would be our new way of life, and it started before we even left on the day of our move.

We were living in a basement apartment at the time, so decided to bring everything upstairs and outside onto the lane so that when the moving truck showed up, we could load it up quite quickly. Hours went by and there was still no truck. For some reason it was not showing up, so we called to see what was going on. The response was a quick sorry, and an explanation of how there were too many people needing the trucks that day so we needed to give it a few days. Give it a few days? Our lease was up so there was no going back into the apartment, and we were definitely not up for camping in the lane with a whole apartment full of contents. Certainly, it would have been nice for them to tell us ahead and not confirm our booking days earlier if they couldn't provide the truck! Fortunately, after a conversation that Jeff had with the company, they decided that there was a truck to spare and sent it over. A few hours later, we were on our way to our new apartment in Toronto.

My parents had agreed to make the 2-hour drive from their home to meet us there so they could help us with unloading.

When we arrived at the apartment, the strangest thing happened. The people who previously rented the apartment weren't ready to move out. The landlord told us that he had asked them to leave, but that they did not want to yet and needed a few days. We couldn't believe it! How do you not move out of your rental when your lease is over and there are people in the lane from another city waiting to move in? We talked further to the landlord regarding the situation, but he made it clear he had no intentions of forcing these renters out and offered us another apartment instead. He said we could stay in that apartment until the people were ready to leave. I still can't believe to this day that we agreed to this offer, as we had no guarantee that this arrangement would meet our needs and that we would be settled and ready for Jeff to be at his job two days later. We were setting ourselves up for disaster.

The second rental was in the same building, but two flights up. As we walked into it, I was mortified! The people that left had trashed the place and no one cleaned up after them. It was so filthy that we couldn't take our shoes off or even use the kitchen to cook. The apartment was in absolute shambles, but we decided to stay as we had nowhere else to go. We tried to be positive about our experience so far, believing that things were going to get better and this was just temporary.

Unfortunately, things did not get better, as we were living in one of the worst locations in Toronto where crime and sexual assault were an everyday occurrence. We didn't know this before we moved and had no time to research prior to our move. I heard gunshots go off the second week of our stay and later learned that a lady had been shot on her front lawn. Not long after, I had gone to the pharmacy for something, and when I walked in, there were guards standing around with guns. It felt like I was in the movies. It seemed so surreal. Why would guards with guns be needed in a pharmacy? I was unfamiliar with such a scene having been raised in a small town and then living in a smaller city where I felt safe most of the time.

There was another odd occurrence a few days after we moved in that happened when I went to a gym nearby to look into getting a membership. I was standing by a pay phone when a man walked up and asked me how to use it. I was so naive and didn't clue in at all that the man had no interest in the phone. As I started to very gently explain to him how to use it, he began to move towards me closer and closer until I felt extremely uncomfortable and became fearful. I walked away and he began to follow me so I ran as fast as I could into my car and slammed down the locks with him right behind me.

This was the beginning of a downward spiral into fear and anxiety.

Two weeks later, the tenants in the first apartment we rented decided to finally move out and my parents traveled two hours again to help us move our contents down the two flights. We quickly got things set up so we could get started on our life in the big city with hopeful expectation, but after the first week of being there, we noticed a trend that we weren't enjoying very much. There were people in our backyard most evenings doing street drugs while their young children ran around till late at night. Talking to the landlord about it proved futile as he refused to confront them due to fear. Needless to say, I began to feel more and more unsafe by the day. If the landlord was too terrified to talk to these tenants, we certainly weren't interested in doing it either. Many nights I would peek out our bedroom window to see what was going on and have Jeff sternly warn me to get away from the window and not move in case they saw me. Who knows what they would have done if they did!

At this point, I was living in a state of constant stress and fear which was about to take its toll on me.

Then one afternoon as I was walking around in the kitchen, I began to suddenly feel extremely sick to my stomach. Nausea wasn't normal for me so it caught me off guard a little. However, it was the least of my worries as the next thing I knew, I felt I couldn't breathe properly. Then my body started to shake inside and a terror enveloped me so strongly that I was sure I was dying. I ran outside thinking that some fresh air would help, but it didn't. Then I tried to read some bible verses to calm myself down, but that did not help either. I began to hyperventilate and assumed I would pass out any minute, but after a few minutes it passed and I began to feel normal again, other than being very shaky and weak. I had no idea what had just happened to me and I was terrified it would happen again. It especially concerned me that it might happen while at work or in public. Up to that point, I had never heard of a panic attack and certainly had no idea there was treatment for this kind of thing, which only added to the fear.

I began to feel on edge most of the time, shaking inside and feeling this awful fear that something bad was going to happen. Then I would find myself crying at times for no reason, which was definitely not normal for me. While this was all going on, Jeff had switched his job, as it was extremely stressful and not what he had envisioned at all. I was working as a hairstylist in a shop where the boss wasn't sure if he was hiring me or not. We were only two months into our move, but the extreme changes that we were experiencing were proving too much for us to handle.

Chapter 4

OUT OF CONTROL

As time went on, Jeff and I seemed to barely see each other, as the days and evenings were taken up not only working but getting to our jobs and back. The morning routine for both of us included walking to a bus stop, taking the bus to the subway station, and walking to our jobs after taking the subway. I personally felt like I had a very good workout by the time I got to work. When we were together for that hour or so before bed, we would sit in fear of the people outside so it was not exactly quality time.

After 2 months, we decided we needed to move as neither one of us was enjoying anything anymore including our jobs.

Before the next move however, Jeff decided to leave his job as he wasn't able to cope with the constant pressures from his boss. We assumed he wouldn't have a problem finding something similar but we were wrong. Getting another job wasn't as easy as we thought it would be so in desperation he took on a commission job as a vacuum cleaner salesman. I will never forget the day that I sat on the couch and watched as Jeff practiced his vacuum cleaner demonstration for me for the first time. It felt like I was in the Twilight zone as I watched and listened to him. I couldn't have imagined our lives would come to this if I tried. I had also left my job around this time because, after two weeks, the boss still hadn't paid me and couldn't decide whether or not he wanted to hire me.

Financially we were suffering so I decided that I would try and ease the burden by taking on a job delivering Yellow Page books around Toronto while I looked for another hair styling job. I knew nothing about driving in a big city but had no choice except to figure it out and there was no GPS to help. Memories of me thumping over the streetcar tracks with a car full of heavy books still haunt me today.

Both of us felt defeated and devastated as this was not what we signed up for when we left everything to come to Toronto.

We ended up leaving the apartment and moving to another part of the city only to experience similar issues there with tenants not wanting to move out and unstable neighbors. I didn't know it at the time, but I was on my way to a horrific mental breakdown.

The panic attacks would happen on and off and I would cry on and off daily. The worst thing was that I started to lose complete control over my thoughts. I would have nagging, repetitive negative thoughts go through my head all day and couldn't stop them no matter what I did. The thoughts were always negative which was challenging enough, but then they got to a point where they were always about death. I began to lose my appetite which led to extreme weight loss, and I lived in terror every day of losing my mind completely. Although I shared some of my symptoms with a friend, I didn't share much of it with Jeff or anyone else as I thought they would not understand and judge me. And besides, I did not want to add any more stress to Jeff's life as I knew he was struggling too. He had also been traumatized by his mother's suicide when he was just three, so there was no way that I was going to share with him what was going on in my mind.

During this time, I started to think about my grandmother a lot and wondered if my worst fear was coming to pass. What if I had what she did and would have to be sent to some mental hospital somewhere? What would people think of me then? I could barely handle the thought and it just added to all the other stress and fear I was carrying.

Somehow through all of this, I found another hairstyling job in a very high end salon. At first, I felt excited about the downtown location and the upscale image that the salon seemed to portray. However, I learned very quickly that looks mean nothing. I was used to being friendly back in Kingston with the goal of building a clientele, and here I was working with a boss who would reprimand me for smiling. The first week at work he said to me " you can put your smile away because these people don't give a hell about you." I was in shock! The salon charged an extra ten dollars if a client requested you and the extra charge was to discourage them from this as my boss feared hairdressers would take clients with them when they moved on. To me, this seemed irrational as a salon in a city like Toronto with a population of over 2,500,000 should not have to fight to keep clients. Because I was not an oppositional person by nature, I just went along with whatever the boss would tell me though it annoyed me.

Jeff was able to put the vaccum sales days behind him when a new job offer came along. We were hopeful that finally we were going to get a break but unfortunately his job experiences continued to just add to the stress in our lives. His boss was extremely demanding and would expect him to work ten-hour shifts and make him feel horrible if he occasionally left after nine hours which he attempted to do on my birthday.

I still tried to have a good attitude and forced myself to spend time with others, thinking that it might distract me enough and get rid of whatever this uncontrollable problem I had was. Unfortunately, it did nothing to ease any of my sufferings but actually made it worse because I was reminded of how abnormal I was. Why could I not get a grip? I had been so used to controlling my emotions in the past, but now I couldn't control a thing. I tried everything in my power to get rid of the horrible feelings and thoughts. There was no relief to be found anywhere. Finally, after my third salon job, I told Jeff that I couldn't handle living there anymore and wanted to move back to Kingston. He was more than happy to move back as he was on his second headhunting job at the time and even though he was done with the vacuum cleaners, he was still not coping well. We decided that because I could probably get a job quicker, I would move back first and secure an apartment. He would join me once I had a job so at least one of us was working. I was so happy that he was on board with this, as I honestly did not think I could take another day where we had no supports. I felt that moving back would fix everything and that I would quickly snap out of whatever was wrong with me. So moving is exactly what we did. I was able to get a hairstyling job quite quickly, and a month later, Jeff moved back from Toronto and joined me. The only problem was that the horrible symptoms I had been experiencing were not going away.

I began to share a little of what was going on with a few other people in spiritual authority, hoping they would say, "Oh don't worry, I've had that happen too. It will go away," but this was not the case. The responses I got were without any depth of understanding of what I was going through. "You just need to read your bible more," or "You just need to speak out loud positive declarations that you are healed, and you will be," were what I heard them say. I was so desperate and vulnerable that I did whatever people told me to do. I remember sitting on a chair one day saying over and over again that I was healed while trying to believe with all my might that I was, but the symptoms were only getting worse as I was now starting to feel heavy guilt and shame on top of everything else. Why was my faith not strong enough to ward off these symptoms? At this point, I felt my mind was going to snap any minute. Some of the panic attacks were so severe that I began to lose my sight and hearing. It was obvious something was seriously wrong with me and just speaking out loud that I was healed was not the solution. I barely had the strength to believe anything anymore and couldn't concentrate to even read two sentences. I felt like I was trapped in a bubble, alone, full of fear, helpless, and with no hope of ever being the happy, fun person I once was.

You might wonder at this point how Jeff was coping with all of this, watching his normally happy, contented, passionate, and "full of life" wife morphing into a shell of herself.

Jeff had actually had his own experience with mental illness before all this and had been hospitalized for a year when he was twenty years old. He had suffered from a psychotic breakdown and depression along with trying to take his own life a number of times. Sadly, Jeff had inherited the genetic predisposition to the imbalance that his mother suffered with. For Jeff, the imbalance was triggered by drugs and alcohol which he had involved himself with quite regularly as a teen. After the doctors were able to get Jeff's mind leveled out on the right medications and he was well enough, a Christian couple took him into their home after he was discharged to help him recover. At the time the hospital provided families that were available for this purpose. What a gift they were to him and so many others they helped in this way.

One weekend they invited Jeff to a Christian festival. He wasn't interested at first until they told him there would be amazing guitar players in the bands. Because Jeff had always loved to play the bass guitar, this intrigued him. Little did he know that his decision to go that day would change his life! During one of the concerts, Jeff had a supernatural experience that he describes was like a bolt of electricity that went through him. He says it was an amazing feeling, not fearful, but instead, very peaceful. Since he was not using any drugs other than prescribed medication, he knew it was not drug-related. He was convinced that he was touched by God at that moment and healed miraculously from a chemical imbalance.

I had met Jeff soon after this festival and remember him mentioning that he had been taking a number of pills every day because he had an imbalance, but that he felt like he didn't need them anymore. Having no knowledge of the types of medications he was on and how chemical imbalances worked, I gladly agreed with him, as he looked quite normal to me. As he began to wean himself off the medications, I received a visit from a hospital nurse. She was completely opposed to him going off his medication and kept trying to convince me that it was not a good idea. I would just say to her, "You don't understand….he doesn't need it!" I think it went in one ear and out the other as she started to talk about how many of the patients had spiritual experiences and it was all part of the illness. I didn't listen to anything she said, and thankfully so, as if this had happened later on in our lives with everything I know now, I would be agreeing with her wholeheartedly and begging Jeff not to adjust anything!

I believe that Jeff definitely received a miracle that day as he was able to get off his medication easily and was able to go years without it. This is definitely not the norm for people who are on these types of medications, so there is no other logical explanation as to why he was able to do this except for the fact that it truly was a miraculous healing.

Even though Jeff had suffered from a mood disorder in the past, he didn't seem to quite understand how to help me. In his mind, coming at it solely from a spiritual angle should have been the answer. In my worst panic attacks, he would say, "Let's just sit down and pray," while I was running around out of control yelling at him to call an ambulance, as I was sure I was dying. He obviously loved me deeply and wanted nothing more than to help me, but became frustrated at how little progress there was. He had to learn that not everyone had the blessing of instant healing and recovery. Most people had a journey of ups and downs in order to find this kind of healing. I would be one of these people whether we liked it or not.

Chapter 5

SEEKING HELP

We had lived in Toronto for about 5 months before I moved back on my own to Kingston to look for an apartment and a job.

I was fortunate to find a job quickly and it involved being a hairstylist in a brand new hair salon. I liked the idea of this because to me it felt like a new beginning- maybe I would be able to leave the past behind and finally move on to new and better things. Just maybe I was going to experience freedom from whatever hole I was in with this new season of my life.

I didn't understand that there was actually a chemical imbalance going on in my brain at this point and that it wasn't going to just disappear overnight or in the next few months for that matter. I did my best to pretend I was happy and relaxed while I worked but I would find myself having to leave my clients to run to the staff room to work myself through a panic attack quite often. I was also extremely emotional in my car on the way to work and on the way home when I felt I could let my guard down and cry again. This was all extremely irritating to me because I wanted so desperately to be normal and get on with my life but my body and mind wouldn't let me.

The emotional toll on me caused me to make mistakes in my hair styling that I had never made in the past. Even though I tried with all of my might to do my job well, my boss was noticing some of my struggles and recognized that I was very sick. She had experience with major depression in the past so recognized it in me. After three months of me working in her salon, she came to me and said that she was laying me off so I could go to a doctor and get proper help.

At first, I was devastated at the thought of not being able to work, something I had done since I was twelve years old. I didn't know what to do with myself and felt completely alone as I laid around most of the days with my head spinning uncontrollably, wondering what was wrong with me and questioning why I wasn't getting any better. I actually didn't go to the doctor at first because I allowed people to convince me to believe that if I just prayed harder or read my Bible more, things would change for the better. Some people were also suggesting that I keep speaking positive words out loud about how healthy I was in hopes that it would change me. I'm all for positive talk but when a person is in the midst of a serious depressive episode, this is too much to expect as it just feels like one big lie. The reality is that positive words alone will not fix a chemical imbalance in the brain.

One day, my friend Karen Bandy came over to see me when she heard how sick I was, with a booklet by a man named Dr. Grant Mullen. While reading it, I clued in very quickly that this man was a man of faith who believed in the power of prayer, yet encouraged people to get medical help because he was a psychiatrist and understood the brain. This man explained how mood disorders were a chemical imbalance in the brain that needed medication to balance them out. He had a checklist of symptoms in the book for a number of mood disorders including depression, anxiety, bipolar, schizophrenia, and panic disorders. I went through the checklists, and under depression, anxiety, and panic disorder, I had every single symptom.

You would think this would have frightened me further, but after months of not knowing what was happening to me, to see that these terrible symptoms finally had names and that they were treatable, gave me a glimmer of hope.

This man also explained how people of faith can actually suffer a lot worse than others because they have the guilt and shame of not being able to "believe" or "pray" themselves out of it, as well as trying to cope with insomnia, anxiety, deep sadness that never goes away, and the stigma that often comes along with these types of illnesses. It was amazing to read the booklet, as it felt like a huge load of guilt had been lifted off of me that day. He totally understood what I was going through and encouraged medication, which is what I needed to hear at such a challenging time. As I read his words, my thinking shifted and clarity began to enter my broken brain. It was ok that I was a person of faith and needed medication! God would not strike me dead for having a "lack of faith!" He actually wanted me well and created doctors and medication to help me. It was the enemy of my soul who wanted me to suffer endlessly and remain sick. It sounds so simple and yet up until then, the guilt associated with taking a medication was massive. The lights were going on and I was finally getting it, kind of.

I decided to go to the doctor soon after these revelations but I was very anxious about what the doctors approach to medicate me would be. I had barely taken any medication in my life up to this point and was raised with home remedies when help was needed. I don't ever remember my mom handing us medication when we were younger and sick, but I do remember taking cod liver oil and brewer's yeast. It must have worked well because we seemed to cope just fine back then without all the drugs we see on the market today!

After listening to my situation, not surprisingly, the doctor diagnosed me with major depression and anxiety disorder. I was sent home with prescriptions for an antidepressant, a sleeping pill, and an anti-anxiety pill. She explained that the anti-anxiety pill would give me quick relief if I was having a panic attack, but the antidepressant could take four to six weeks to work and there were possible side effects to be aware of. The worst news of all was that there was no guarantee the medication was even going to work. There were many different ones available and it would be by trial and error that the right one would be found for me. After I heard this I was beyond discouraged as I couldn't imagine having to wait so long or have this not work. I could barely handle one more hour of what felt like torture. I had suicidal thoughts in the past on and off throughout this whole ordeal, but they attacked me with a vengeance now. How was I going to survive all this when I already felt like I was holding on by a thread? I was very nervous about it all but felt I had no option as it was getting harder and harder to cope with everyday life. It was time to get my life back, and if this was my best chance, I had to try it.

Thank goodness Jeff had moved back in with me before I started my new medication. I needed the support then more than ever!

Unfortunately, the first medicine was not a good match for me, as the side effects were too difficult for me to deal with. I couldn't cope with much so possibly the nausea felt worse than it really was, but the insomnia was unbearable. I was not sleeping at all. The drug kept me up all night long for three days and two nights and this was after taking double doses of sleeping pills. Sleeplessness to that degree does not help the recovery process at all. To add insult to injury, I was going to my family doctor for all of this and it seemed to me that she was not confident at all in what she was doing. She would take the pamphlet out of the sample pill box and start reading through it after looking up the drug in a reference book. This did not make me feel very safe. I felt I needed to ask for a referral to a psychiatrist which was extremely hard for me as it was another reminder of how sick I really was. Never in my life did I think I would be going to a head doctor!

My doctor agreed it would be a good idea to refer me on so she sent the referral forward. It took a few weeks to get in but it was definitely the right thing to do as I was able to have a thorough assessment done and would be monitored by someone who specialized in mood disorders. After our first meeting, I received the diagnosis of anxiety and major depressive disorder once again. I was glad to hear the diagnosis confirmed by someone in the field, and it made me feel a little more confident about trying another medication. The psychiatrist gave me a new medication but also recommended I see a psychologist. To me, this was absolutely ridiculous. Why on earth would I go see someone like that? To talk about what? Those professionals were for people who needed serious help and were messed up. That was not me. I just needed some pills to fix my brain chemicals then I would be fine.

The good news is that the next medication I tried had few side effects and worked well. It took a few weeks, but finally, I started to feel hope that I might be able to function normally again someday. As the weeks went on I found myself crying less, feeling less nervous, sleeping better, being more active, and feeling joy again. After six months I was fully functional again and had even started my own traveling hairstyling business. I called it "Hair I

Come" as I would travel to my clients' homes to do their hair for them. The business grew quickly as there were only a few stylists in the city doing this type of work. I loved my job. The pay was great and most of my clients were extremely thankful for my services. During this time Jeff was working for a wonderful insurance company in the city. We bought our first house together and felt like the past was finally behind us.

A few years later when we were both twenty-seven, we decided that we wanted to start having children. We were beyond excited and felt extremely blessed to find out I was pregnant soon after we made the decision. I didn't feel good about being on an antidepressant while being pregnant, however, and because I was doing so well for so long, I decided that it was time for me to wean off. I talked to the psychiatrist about it, but he cautioned me, saying that I would be very vulnerable to postpartum depression and it might be a good idea to stay on it. In my thinking, the past was the past and I didn't need medication anymore. I was going to be completely fine without the medication and it couldn't possibly be healthy for me to be on them long term anyway, I reasoned.

I should have known something was off when my moods were unusually up and down through the whole pregnancy. The nausea I had the first three months was almost unbearable. I could hardly eat at all and had lost ten pounds by the end of the third month which made me very weak and anxious. I assumed some mood swings were normal. I started eating again in the fourth month, and other than the normal discomforts of pregnancy, I felt much better until the labor started at forty weeks. I endured sixty hours of labor, was completely exhausted, and wondering if I would live through it before I finally begged for an epidural. In my experience with this labour, hot showers, rolling on balls, water needles in the back, and gas masks, proved to be distractions rather than helps, and offered no actual pain relief. We had a midwife so my care had to be transferred to a doctor in order for me to receive the epidural. I was extremely thankful to be able to get the epidural quite quickly and finally have some relief.

After two hours of pushing, my precious baby girl entered the world. My husband and I had never felt so much joy in our lives. There were some minor physical complications with me after the birth, but nothing that kept me from enjoying every minute with her. I felt wonderful mentally and believed the worst was behind me. Unfortunately, I was wrong.

Two months later, all the symptoms of depression and anxiety crept back in. I kept thinking it was just the "baby blues," and that everyone felt this way after a baby. A few more weeks went by and things got worse and worse. Once again I felt like I was losing my mind as I couldn't control anything I was thinking about and began to have terrifying thoughts that consumed me night and day. I began to feel detached from my daughter which really frightened me as I felt so close those first few weeks. The anxiety was now keeping me up at night even when my baby was sleeping and I lost all interest in things I used to love like people and food. Everything became an effort and I could barely get out of bed anymore. The nagging negative thoughts caused me to imagine the front cover of a newspaper with my picture and the words, "mother goes insane and harms her child". I had heard stories in the past of this happening and in my mind there was no reason why I couldn't be the next out of control mother. The thoughts were unbearable. After a few more weeks I finally realized and accepted that I needed medical help again as time was not healing a thing. So after four months of nursing, I quit cold turkey to go on an antidepressant as I didn't feel peaceful about being on the medicine and nursing. I was extremely sad that I had to give it up but I knew the priority was my mental health. Once again I began the journey to recovery.

As I began to recover, I started to read more as I was determined to figure out why this happened to me again. I felt there was something I was missing, even after all I had read in Grant Mullen's book about mood disorders. I blamed myself for not having a full understanding of what went wrong and thought if I could just figure out the one root issue, it would solve everything. I felt I was responsible for what was happening to me and that there must have been something I was doing wrong in order for this ailment to afflict me once again.

One day as I began to read a book on depression, it talked about how depression was often a result of buried anger. I was so angry when I read this because I was the happiest person I knew when I was well. I didn't have buried anger! How silly! It amazes me now how closed I was to certain ideas because I had no understanding of them and wanted to believe what I wanted to believe. I did not know that there were many roots to depression and anxiety and that treatment was never just one silver bullet, but many bullets. It was vital to look for and be open to the possibility of many roots to the depression and anxiety.

At the time, because I wasn't open to many suggestions on what could be causing my depression, I decided once again to believe that my only hope was medication. It wasn't easy and it took time, but the medication did do its job and I eventually returned to the healthy and happy self I once was. I had no idea that I could actually become an even healthier, happier person, or that there even was such a thing for me, but there was. It would take time, but it would happen down the road.

The doctor had told me at this time that I needed to stay on the medicine for life as a preventative measure as there was a great risk I could have another episode if I went off it, and that each episode would be worse and take longer to heal from. It was extremely difficult for me to accept this as there was still something in me that believed medication for a mood disorder was not a good thing. It didn't help that people would say to me that "medicine was just a crutch," or that it was a "bandaid covering up the real problems". This made me feel uneasy for years. I felt caught between believing what the mental health professionals were saying and what others were saying. It felt like my soul, body, and spirit were at war with each other and it would be years before they would be at peace.

I decided to listen to the doctor and stay on the medication even though everything in me wanted to get off. I knew that the medicines had toxins in them for one thing and so I would picture the chemicals in the medicine destroying every one of my organs as it moved its way down my digestive tract. Yes, I was a little dramatic and extreme in my view of things, however, it was something that bothered me deeply and it made me hate the idea of having to ingest them every day. Because of this I tried to restrict their use and to take the least amount possible. Then I read Dr. Grant Mullen's advice from a book he wrote that said, "you want to take the right dose, not the least amount." I remember thinking, "Well, that makes sense. Would someone take half their insulin if they had diabetes?" That convinced me to take what I needed even though it made me cringe. However, it dawned on me that I did not have to be helpless, but that there were things I could do to protect my body from the toxins. My liver was my biggest concern as there were warnings on the medication information literature about possible liver damage caused by its use and I was having my liver tested on a regular basis to keep an eye on it. I will share later on what I discovered regarding protecting the body from toxins.

Finally, I accepted the idea that at this time I needed the

medications I was on. It was a season, and in time, I would be able to reduce and even discontinue some of the medicines. This is something that I would encourage anyone taking these types of medicines to remember. There is always the possibility that the number of medications and dose amounts can be adjusted over time as recovery continues.

As my brain began to heal from the imbalance, I was able to get off the sleeping pills as I started sleeping properly again without them. Then I found myself needing the anti-anxiety medication less and less until one day I didn't need it anymore. I was then only on a low dose of the antidepressant which I was so grateful for.

The next ten years were wonderful to me. I stayed on medication to have my son almost three years after my daughter was born, which resulted in no major mood issues. Even though there were normal stresses with raising two children, supporting my husband in his career, and running a household, I felt like I could handle it all, as my mind was healthy and life was enjoyable for the most part. It was a perfect balance of enjoying time with my family and friends and playing sports which I loved.

In the summer of 2011 however, things began to change.

Chapter 6

ANOTHER BREAKDOWN

Jeff and I had always noticed some challenges with our son since he was young, but they seemed to be growing bigger by the day. We wondered if there was something more going on, besides just a demanding, strong-willed boy, but we had no idea what. Since the day Elijah could walk, he was always a super active little guy who kept me in pretty good shape. He was a ball of energy who needed a challenge at all times or he would get bored very quickly and get into mischief when possible. He loved to be close to me at all times as well, so he would follow me around the house most of the day, hoping I would entertain him. Often I would, which was exhausting because he was not interested in the regular play that most boys were. At five years old, instead of sitting and playing with cars, Elijah was building massive ball machines in his bedroom with trap doors and tunnels with KNEX building kits. KNEX are made up of many pieces, mostly gears, blocks, small and large plastic pins, and wheels. My job was to organize all the pieces and colors for him and hand them to him when needed.

KNEX became a huge interest of his which meant we made a lot of ball machines.

Elijah was very particular about his food and would gag often if the texture or taste wasn't just right. When he was two, he went through a phase where he was extremely interested in the alphabet and spent hours with letters. He would draw bubble letters and color them in different patterns, then move onto his alphabet puzzles which he completed over and over again. He wanted letters incorporated into everything, so we had alphabet cookie cutters, cereal, and pasta among other things. Since Elijah was so particular about his food and getting the right foods into him was such a chore, I came up with a bright idea of carving some of his foods into alphabet letters, and it worked! I would carve his cheese and toast into letters every day to get them into his diet. It's the only way he would eat it. Amazingly he would remember what letter we were on each day. If I carved the same letter as the day before, he would be very upset and not eat until I carved the right one.

When I look back now, all this is fascinating and even comical to me, however, at the time I was so tired, frustrated, and constantly stressed out that I could not enjoy it. I read every book I could find about how to properly parent such a strong-willed child. Little did we know that we were dealing with an incredibly bright child who actually had Aspergers, ADHD, and was gifted academically. When we had his assessment done in 2015, at the age of 10, Elijah received his diagnosis along with being called a "genius" by the child psychologist. No wonder I was worn ragged all the time! Everything finally made sense and I will be forever thankful for the revelation we received about our incredible son that summer! He amazes me to this day and brings me great joy even though there is also much stress involved in parenting a child who fluctuates between young and immature to old and wise many times on a daily basis.

In 2011 Jeff had decided to make a career move and start his own mortgage business. I felt that it was a great idea as he had years of experience in the insurance industry and two years in the mortgage industry. We both felt complete peace in moving forward with it. At the time I was not working outside the home so this was a huge leap of faith for us.

As the business began, new stresses also began. Even though we were trying our best to trust that everything would work out, the reality of running a new business set in. The expenses were much higher than what we had anticipated and the stress was taking a huge toll on Jeff. This also took a toll on me along with the challenges that were escalating with Elijah. I was trying to keep up relationships with several friends, give our daughter, Lydia, the time she needed with me, play sports, do some hair on the side to bring in a little income, host a playgroup every week, and be part of a busy church team which I all thoroughly enjoyed. I was used to being an active, busy person and I loved people, so any opportunities to be involved with them was too difficult for me to give up. I felt quite fulfilled even though I was often exhausted and coffee became one of my best friends.

It was the summer of 2012 when I started to notice some unexpected anxiety. When this anxiety crept up, I was a little irritated with it. I figured it would go away soon so just tried to get through the days and took anti-anxiety pills when I needed to. It seemed to come and go for a couple of months and I wasn't able to put my finger on why it was happening. This really frustrated me as I'm the type of person who likes to figure things out and know why they are happening. Because I was not able to figure it out, I would find myself so angry that I would get teary-eyed, and then that would make me angry! It's ridiculous to me now looking back how I could think I had no anger. I actually had a lot of it buried deep inside but had no idea it was there.

Once again I began to experience some feelings of depression, a feeling I did not want to relive. Even though ten years had gone by without it, it took about two minutes to remember that horrible, heavy cloud. I was determined not to focus on any of it and just continue my day to day activities like usual which I found was not going to work very well. Soon I began to avoid situations where I felt like I would have to fake feeling good because it was too tiring. Happy people started to irritate me and church became a chore. I still would go, but would sit there the whole time annoyed with everything and everyone, including God. Many of the songs we sang made me irritable as I was in no mood to be singing in the first place.

Talking to anyone about what I was feeling was out of the question because I didn't want to give the awful feelings any extra attention, but instead tried everything I could to get rid of them. I didn't tell Jeff much how I felt because I didn't want him worrying and hid it completely from my children to protect them.

There was one night in particular that I remember when Jeff and I went over for dinner to the home of a couple we loved to spend time with. We had met Bonnie and Roger Rutter about five years prior to this evening. They were quite a few years older than us, but we had many things in common, so developed a wonderful friendship. They had become mentors to us as well which we were very grateful for. Roger and Jeff seemed to have similar personalities and enjoyed talking about business amongst other common interests. Bonnie was as sweet as pie and still is one of the most gentle people I know. She made me feel safe very quickly in our friendship, however, she had never seen me in a depressive state or full of anxiety, so I tried hard to hide it in fear that she might look at me differently if she knew I was struggling emotionally. However, as the evening went on, the feelings of fear and sadness got too intense and began to creep out of me. I had to tell her what was going on. She was very supportive and even said a prayer for me, yet I still felt embarrassed about being so emotional. Strangely, I also felt some relief shortly after because I was able to be real and let her see my weakness, if only for a moment.

Unfortunately, things continued to get worse, and there was no forgetting about any of this. The growing symptoms started to consume my thoughts most of the day. I knew then that I needed to go to a doctor somewhere to get my medication adjusted or changed as something was not working properly. At this point, my state of health had become obvious to others and a friend suggested I go to see a psychiatrist that she had dealt with in the past. I didn't have a regular psychiatrist at this time as I had not needed one for years, so I decided to go to the doctor my friend had recommended. I took another friend with me to my first appointment as she too was struggling with some anxiety issues. We thought we would kill two birds with one stone and make a day trip out of it as it was an hour away. I'm so glad I took my friend as she is one of those people who can always find something to laugh about, even in a situation like this. Because laughter had always been one of my biggest coping mechanisms, we made quite the pair. In between bouts of tears and medication popping, we would laugh at anything we found funny.

Laughter truly can be good medicine, and in this case, the dose was exactly what I needed to get through the day.

When we got to our destination, we were checked in and called in separately to meet Dr. Jack. He was a friendly, elderly man who made me feel comfortable right from the start. After some small talk, he asked me to fill out a simple questionnaire so he could see what he was dealing with. It was no surprise that the results showed that I was struggling with anxiety and some low-grade depression. After his eyes were done scanning the pages, he looked up and started to talk to me about my emotions. He specifically asked me how I had dealt with emotions in the past which I thought was very odd. In my mind, I was there to get a different type of medication so I could feel normal again and get on with my life. I didn't quite understand why we were now talking about emotions. I was convinced that the anxiety I was feeling had nothing to do with the fact that I had stuffed certain emotions down for over thirty years. I just had a bit of a chemical imbalance again and needed another pill to fix it!

I listened to the doctor talk about how stress affects the body and how repressed emotions can cause physical and mental health problems. He got out his pointer stick and started pointing at a big picture of an iceberg that he had shone on the wall with his projector. The picture showed the top of an iceberg above the water and the bottom of it under the water. The top portion was much smaller than the ice under water. As he pointed to the picture he said, "Now this is what happens to us when we repress emotions. The top part represents what we are showing, the happy-go-lucky, laid-back, in-control self, but the hidden part represents the anger, rage, frustration, sadness, and disappointment that is buried underneath. It is huge when we don't deal with it because it doesn't go away but continues to just pile up. In time, if not expressed, the body starts to react when it can't handle any more buried emotion. It starts to break down from the stress of it all." The doctor continued to explain that this kind of stress can affect everyone in different ways, that some people get illnesses like fibromyalgia or arthritis, and others get mental illnesses and that the body will give out where it is vulnerable and vulnerability can come from genetics or the environment amongst other things.

For some reason, I was still not in a place to receive any of this message and didn't want to hear it. Maybe it sounded too uncomfortable or like too much work to me, I'm not sure, but I became very annoyed at the whole idea. I was getting very irritated with the doctor as all I wanted was a prescription, not a lecture on why he thought I was the way I was. He even handed me a pack of CDs on the subject to listen to at home which I was in no frame of mind to do. I took them home only because I didn't want to hurt his feelings, after all, I was a people pleaser. Finally, after an hour of powerpoint slides, questionnaires, and Dr. Jack sharing all his "emotional" wisdom, I finally was given my new prescription. In my mind, that was all I needed to get better, and hopefully, I would never have this problem again.

It's amazing how we can believe what we want to believe and not necessarily what the truth is.

There seemed to be some improvement for a few months on the new medicine, but then one morning I woke up while on vacation with my family in Florida and knew something was horribly wrong. I felt completely flat like a robot and full of fear because I knew I had gone backward in my recovery. I managed to get through the week, but when I got back to Kingston, I felt like I was holding on by a thread. My mind was constantly spinning, and horrible, negative thoughts consumed my mind all day long once again. I could not turn them off no matter what I did. It had been a long time since I had felt this way, but my memory was refreshed very quickly and it was terrifying. The thoughts were really starting to frighten me as they were once again often related to death and not being able to live anymore. Hopelessness crept in more and more and all I could do was wonder if I would ever get well again. The medications seemed to work so well in the past. What on Earth was going on? Why were they not working now?

The next month was spent trying to pretend that I was normal when it was so far from the truth. I had been experiencing these awful symptoms for only a month, but it felt like years, as I slowly began to forget any of my good years and focused only on the negative times when I was sick. It was all consuming, and once again I was in that bubble of darkness where I couldn't find relief anywhere. I was desperate and felt that my only hope for any quick help was to go down to the emergency department at the hospital. So in January of 2012, I drove myself down to the emergency department totally relying on the staff there to get me the help I needed. Jeff still had no idea how badly I was struggling or I know he would have taken me. I walked into the emergency room and was so weak and tired that I couldn't think straight at all. I was crying on and off and trembling while explaining to the triage nurse that I was having horrible thoughts. I assumed when she saw how I looked and acted, she would have put me to the top of the list and that someone would whisk me away somewhere for help right away. Instead, I was put in a room by myself for a few hours with a box of Kleenex so I could cry alone in privacy. I'm assuming they were doing this to lessen the embarrassment for me which was somewhat thoughtful, but being alone was horrible.

After a wait of three hours, a doctor finally showed up to tell me that they couldn't do anything at the hospital except book an appointment with one of the psychiatrists there for two weeks away. They couldn't even adjust my medication! I could not believe what I was hearing. Earlier when they had asked me if I was having suicidal thoughts, I made it very clear that I did often have such thoughts along with barely being able to function. They must hear this often because it didn't prompt them to action at all. They had no problem sending me home with only a bottle of anxiety medication and a card with the mental health crisis phone number on it. In my opinion, this is a terrible way to treat someone so desperate for help. I have heard many stories since of people going to a hospital emergency room in this condition and being turned away. It seems to me that unless there is blood or a suicide attempt, they don't take it seriously at all. I still don't quite understand why when a person reaches out for help in this state, they are often not helped at all. When you are struggling this badly, holding on for one more day is torturous, let alone waiting two weeks!

I don't know how I hung on while hiding it all from my family, but somehow I did. I did see a psychiatrist from the hospital two weeks later and he not only increased the dose of my medication but added a new one as well. The second was added to try and boost the effects of the first one. It was a crazy, rocky ride for the next six months. I would start to feel better for a few days, then crash for a few more. I was up and down like a yo-yo for those six months all while trying to keep up with the home, being a mom to my kids, wife to my husband, and involved in the church.

At the time our church was hosting an out of town team who came to teach on different subjects like forgiveness, stress, and trauma one weekend a month. I had committed to this team back in the fall when I had been feeling better, but being on the team became more and more difficult. I would often sit in the back and just cry because I was so depressed. The comforting thing is that I didn't stand out too much since many of the people attending would cry on and off on these weekends as the information was hitting home for them. Still, I didn't feel like I had much to offer anyone, but that I was more of a burden than anything, so I kept telling our host team leader that she could ask me to step off at any time and that I would understand. I felt completely unproductive and was just waiting to hear her dismiss me. However, my dear friend Rhonda never did this, but instead kept assuring me that I didn't need to fake a thing, and that I was a help in that I would be able to relate to more people because of my experiences. What a gift!

I will be forever thankful that Rhonda chose to still have me on this team, as I know I would have been even more depressed by being asked to leave. Looking back, I should have asked to take a break until I got well, but I was bound and determined to fight and not allow this unpredictable state to rob more of me than it already had.

In July of the same year, I finally started feeling more stable and felt that I was moving on. My thoughts became more controllable, I felt less anxiety, and I started to have joy again. I was finally feeling hope once again. However, on one of my visits to the pharmacy, I was handed a paper with new research stating that the dose of one of the medicines I was on was causing heart problems in people. This was not what I needed to hear! Heart attacks were extremely prevalent in my family line and this was a stress I didn't want, so at my next appointment with the psychiatrist, I asked to be switched to a prior medication I was on years ago that worked well. He agreed that it would be a good option so we went ahead with it.

I would love to say things went well, but they did not. Finding the right medications for mood disorders can be extremely frustrating, as it's not always a simple process.

I am a huge fan of Dr. Daniel Amen who is the founder of SPECT Imaging in the United States. I have heard him ask the question a number of times, "Why is the brain the only organ that we don't look at before we start medicating it? We would never do this with any other body part." Because of his concern regarding this, he has developed a brain scan where he can see exactly what is going on in the brain and treat it much more accurately.

I have never been offered Dr. Amen's type of treatment anywhere in Canada and I don't know of anyone who has. What a difference this could make in our healthcare system and in the lives of so many people. For now, we are given medicines without seeing inside the brain, and they are tested for their effectiveness by trial and error. I'm really hoping that is going to change soon!

After I started on the older medicine, I became extremely sick once again as the medication was not the right one for the time being. In two months I had lost twenty pounds and was losing all hope again. This time I really felt my life was over. I did not have one more ounce of strength in me to fight this anymore and my thoughts took a turn for the worst. Suicide became a thought that started to make more sense everyday except I didn't want to die! I wanted to live, just not like this!

During this time, I was so thankful to be able to talk often with my close friend Kim over the phone about my situation. She was so good at encouraging me and telling me that things were going to get better. Sometimes we would talk a couple of times a day which is what I seemed to need to survive. I will forever be thankful for her time. Even with our regular talks, the feeling of being completely alone never seemed to go away. I also didn't trust myself to be alone. One day I decided to call my friend Bonnie even though it took every ounce of strength I had. When I first called, she asked if she could come over. I gladly accepted this offer as I knew that I could let her see me for the mess I was, even if it was uncomfortable and it was better than laying there alone with my tormenting, nagging thoughts. Its the hardest thing for a depressed person to reach out as it takes not only a lot of energy but a great deal of vulnerability. However, the benefits are immense.

Even though I felt like I was nothing but a burden to Bonnie at the time with nothing to give back, I still managed to call her numerous times and she graciously was there for me to talk to. She also came over to my house a number of times and would sit on the end of my bed and just listen to me while I cried uncontrollably. She was amazing at just listening and offering a few words of encouragement or prayer without trying to fix the situation and offer all kinds of suggestions. There is definitely a place for suggestions, but in the state, I was in, I was too weak to try anything. I was in a crisis and needed medical intervention as soon as possible. What an incredible gift Bonnie and Kim both were to me in this time!

It wasn't long before I knew I had to tell Jeff the extent of what was going on. I felt like I was having a nervous breakdown and couldn't hold on much longer. In the past I had always tried to protect him, take care of him, making sure all of his needs were met, and did my best to give him a stress-free environment to come home to. Well on this day, I decided that I had to choose my needs over his and not worry about the stress this would cause him if I was going to get well enough to function properly again.

When I called him, I was completely real with him for the first time, and as difficult as it was, there was relief in it. I told him I needed to go to the hospital and get help as I couldn't bear another day of being home alone with my out of control mind. My fear was that he would fall apart and I knew I certainly didn't have the strength to comfort him or say it would be ok. Instead, he was very loving and supportive and came home right away to take me to the hospital.

We didn't want our children to see me in the state I was in so we arranged for a friend to pick them up and take them out. My son was seven at the time and my daughter was ten so we wanted to protect them as much as we could. In our thinking, I would only be gone for a few days to get things straightened out so there was no need to alarm them. Jeff would explain to them later that night that mom needed to go to the hospital for something but would be totally fine and would come home in a few days. Little did we know, this would not be the case at all.

Chapter 7

HOSPITALIZED

The ride to the hospital was horrifying for me. My thoughts wavered from positive to negative. I was hopeful that I would possibly finally get the help I needed, but on the other hand, I couldn't help but grieve the fact that I could no longer provide my family with what they needed. I also had the stress of not knowing if the hospital would even admit me, as they seemed to be very strict with this, and because I wasn't brought in by ambulance, there wasn't any guarantee they would see my situation as an emergency. This is what makes mental illness so difficult..... you can't see it! If someone has a broken bone or gashes on their face from an accident, they are seen immediately, but when there is a broken brain which is mostly invisible to people, it can be difficult to get the help that is needed.

People that knew me well could see there was something seriously wrong as my countenance had completely changed, there was weight loss, and like one friend remarked, the life was completely gone from my eyes.

The doctors at the hospital could only go on what they were told. When we arrived at emergency, I was put in an assessment room where the nurses asked me many questions to see what was going on. I couldn't talk much because I couldn't stop crying. Thankfully, Jeff was excellent at communicating how serious things were. And when the nurse asked, "Is your wife different than she usually is?" instead of giving a long, drawn out answer to her question, he did something very intelligent in my opinion. He took out his IPad to show her a photo of me when I was healthy, grinning from ear to ear, full of life, and said, "This was my wife!" and then he pointed at me sitting on the chair to say, "This is her now!" It didn't take much more convincing after that. They now knew I was very sick.

It was decided at this point that I would be admitted to the psychiatric floor of Kingston General Hospital.

The protocol was that you were put in a wheelchair and a nurse would take you up to the floor. I had never sat in a wheelchair in my life except to jokingly fool around when I was younger, but because I was so weak, I was more than happy to not have to walk down all the corridors, into the elevator, and through the two sets of security alarms before finally reaching the floor, even though it felt very strange. I continued to cry all the way up to the floor.

It was like my body could not hold on any longer and all my emotions were bursting at the seams in every direction. I felt intense fear, anxiety, terror, sadness, hopelessness, despair, and grief all at once. The emotional dams were open and they weren't closing anytime soon. As I was being wheeled down one of the halls, I looked at the wall and noticed a painting hanging there with the word "hope" written in big letters. It meant so much to me at that moment as it was something I wanted so badly. Even though I couldn't see it or feel it at the time, there was hope, and I would feel it again, just not now.

Shortly after arriving, the nurses went through all my belongings and took anything they thought could be a danger to me or other patients. They also took my phone and laptop as they were not allowed in the rooms due to privacy issues. We were allowed to use them in a room with big windows across from the nurses' station but they had to be signed in and out when needed.

I was then brought over to the room I would be staying in. It was very basic with a few shelves and a bed and had a bathroom that I would share with a girl on the other side. The bathroom had a plastic mirror in it, as glass was considered a danger on this floor. This, of course, made perfect sense, as many of the patients had tried to commit suicide before they were admitted.

I don't remember much of my first day at the hospital except that later on in the evening after Jeff had left, I still couldn't stop crying. There was a moment that evening where I looked down at my hospital bracelet then out the window to watch all the people below walking around living their normal lives. I couldn't believe one of my worst fears had come true! I used to be one of those normal people and now here I was in this place, so out of control, I couldn't even remember what normal was.

As I began to unpack my clothing, a nurse came in and asked, "Are you ok? Why are you crying?" I couldn't believe she was asking such a question. I wanted to say, "Well, I'm having a nervous breakdown, I've been petrified of psych wards my whole life and I'm now in one, and I can't be a mom to my kids....must I go on?," but instead I just blurted out that I didn't feel well and was upset about leaving my kids. She said something I don't remember and then went to get a medication for me that would calm me down, something I would get very used to in the days ahead.

The next morning, I had an interview with the psychiatrist and doctors that would be working with me. As I sat there, I couldn't help the tears from falling again so I let them out for all to see. I'll never forget the psychiatrist asking me why I was so upset and me replying, "Because I'm terrified I'll never get better". She then said something that I held onto for weeks. She said, "We're pretty good at getting people better around here". It sounded so simple and yet it was massive for me as it spoke some hope into me again, even if just for a moment.

Words of hope are the greatest gift I feel can be given to someone in such a hopeless state. I needed more than anything to hear that I was going to get well. I needed to somehow believe that this was a season that wouldn't last forever, that I was going to go home again to be with my family, and that I was going to be able to function and feel mentally stable again someday. It was impossible for me to believe it at the time, but I was so desperate to believe it that I held onto any bit of hope I could find.

As fearful as I was being in the hospital at first, it didn't take long for me to get comfortable there. Many different types of people were on the floor with every kind of mental illness including Parkinson's disease, Dementia, Bi-polar, Major depression, anxiety disorders, and even brain injuries. My first few nights were the roughest as there was a man with severe dementia on one side of me who yelled and swore on and off all night long. Another man wandered around in and out of patients' rooms day and night. We were not allowed to close our door as the nurses had to check on us every hour throughout the night. This did not help me to feel safe in any way, but when you have no choice, you succumb to it. I'm so thankful for anxiety and sleeping medications to help us cope when need be. I don't know what I would have done without them.

After a few nights of listening to loud yelling and swearing on and off for hours, I asked if I could be moved to another room as I wasn't getting much sleep. The nurses agreed and put me on the other end of the floor which was wonderful. It was quieter and I was able to sleep much better.

As I became more comfortable with being on the floor and with what I saw and heard, I would find myself often striking up a conversation with someone somewhere. Many depressed patients want to lay in bed and be isolated, but for some reason, I refused to do it. I think the extrovert in me kept wanting to be around people. Even though I felt awful, being around others seemed to divert my attention off myself enough to stay sane. It also provided me with the odd distractions even though they didn't last long. Through my conversations with others, I began to hear their needs and quite naturally started to take care of them to the point that they assumed I was one of the nurses. I would take them for walks, get them their meals, lend them my clothes and would comfort them when they were crying. I even had patients ask me to please get the wandering man out of their bedrooms.

One day, a lady whom I had just met a few days earlier who was very depressed and felt hopeless, put her head on my shoulder and started sobbing uncontrollably as we walked out of a class we attended together. I couldn't help but put my arm around her to try and comfort her even though I was crying too. It actually causes me to giggle now thinking about how ridiculous this must have looked.

For whatever reason, I thrived on seeing and listening to other peoples' issues and trying to fix them. It wouldn't be until at least a year later that I would begin to understand why I had this passion. First of all, I had done it for most of my life starting at an early age with my siblings. I did it for my kids and for my husband and friends without realizing that it was out of balance at times. I didn't know how to receive for myself. It is wonderful to want to give, but when we are not able to receive, we are depleting ourselves, giving out of an empty tank. This is not healthy! I didn't know this at the time, but I sure learned as time went on.

Listening to all the details of the other patients' lives would have affected me negatively enough on a good day, but because of the state I was in, they just amplified my hopelessness and confirmed that there was a slim chance of ever getting well again. I had many people tell me in detail about their abusive traumatic childhoods, the many ways they tried to take their lives, and how their medicines never worked. These things were not helpful for me to listen to when I already felt so hopeless. I needed to hear that I was going to get better and that this wasn't going to continue the rest of my life. I would have benefitted greatly from hearing this every single day!

One morning the doctors came into my room to tell me that they were noticing what I was doing with the other patients. They told me very nicely that I needed to stop worrying about the other patients and focus on getting well myself. I am so thankful they said this to me as I didn't notice the negative effect it was having on me and I needed someone to bring it to my attention.

I wasn't quite sure how to change this habit however as I had taken care of people for so many years that I had no idea how to give that up and just focus solely on myself. Even when people would come to visit me, I would try my best to look like I was okay because I couldn't receive their sympathy or concern. It felt really uncomfortable. However, there were times where I couldn't fake it no matter how hard I tried and I had no choice but to receive in these times. Little did I know that learning how to receive would play a huge role in my recovery.

During this time, I was beyond blessed to have numerous visitors coming in on a daily basis. This was definitely not the norm at all on the psychiatric floor so the staff began to ask me where all the people were coming from. It's not that I was any more important than anyone else, but I had met quite a few people from different churches in the past. Many of these people came to visit. I was so thrilled to tell the staff this because so often the church gets a bad name, however, in this case, the church looked incredible!

The love and compassion that people had for me in this time was overwhelming. Michelle and Grace were two mothers from the school my kids attended who came in almost every day for weeks to see me. I did not know them well but they still chose to grace me with their presence consistently. I had never felt so much love in my life! There were many patients who had never had anyone come in to visit and I actually started feeling guilty that I was getting so much attention. I wasn't good at receiving in the first place, so receiving all this attention was extremely difficult, yet so needed.

There were times I felt like I was on another planet as people visited, especially in those early weeks where I couldn't concentrate and hear what they were saying as my mind wandered constantly, but the love I felt was beyond words. It blew me away. I could barely wrap my mind around the fact that week after week these people would make the effort to come see me, especially knowing that it was a huge ordeal to find parking and go through security twice before finally getting up to the floor. I will be forever grateful!

Jeff and the kids would come to visit me a few times a week but I would meet them downstairs as we wanted the kids protected as much as possible. The visits were really hard for me because I didn't feel like myself at all. The worst part was not feeling connected to my family emotionally and setting the kids up for me to leave them again.

One day as I was getting in the elevator to go back up to my floor, my daughter started crying and begging me to come home. She just kept asking me, "Why can't you come with us mom? Please, mom……" I had to stand there and let the elevator doors close on her so we could once again go our separate ways. It was torture. Every time I had to leave my kids, I would go back to the floor hysterical and the nurses would have to drug me out to calm me down. It was the "not knowing when I would go home" that had me in such a state of grief and sadness. I couldn't say to the kids, "Don't worry guys, mommy will be home next week Wednesday." We couldn't predict anything. It all depended on how the medications were working, and so far they didn't seem to be working at all.

After about a week, I was allowed to go home on a "pass" to try and visit with the family. The nurses warned me that it might be really difficult, and if I needed to come back early, I could. I did not expect it to be as horrible as it was. Everything felt like a trigger and I was constantly reminded of how sick I really was. I hated not feeling connected to Jeff and the kids and it really frightened me. I was constantly trying to hide the tears that were going to fall at any moment and physically I had no strength to even make a meal. I tried my best but couldn't handle it, so I asked Jeff to drive me back to the hospital. You know you're really not well when a psychiatric hospital feels safer to you than your own home, but this is the way it was for me. As soon as I got back to my room at the hospital, I felt safe again. There were no expectations of me. I didn't have to fake anything but could just cry when I needed to, and I didn't have to take care of anyone. All I had to do was worry about myself. How easy, or so I thought!

Three weeks had come and gone and by this time the kids were really upset as they didn't understand why it was taking so long for me to come home. I finally felt that Jeff and I couldn't hide what was going on anymore so I decided to explain in detail to them what was happening with me. On one of my passes home, I had them sit at the table while I got out a piece of paper and pen to draw a diagram of a brain. I explained how we all have chemicals in our brain that help us to feel happy and energetic. I told them I didn't have the right amount of chemicals so I wasn't feeling happy, had no energy, and couldn't do my usual job, but that the doctors were helping me to find a good medicine that would help the chemicals in my brain to work properly. Then I would feel better and come home. I explained how sometimes it takes a little bit of time for them to find the right medicine and for it to work, and even though it was super hard to be apart, that I was in the best place to get the right help. They seemed to understand and accept my explanation even though they were upset that I left so suddenly and they didn't get to say goodbye the day I was admitted. Looking back, I wish I would have been able to explain it to them right at the beginning and say my goodbye, however, I looked so horrible and couldn't stop crying at all so I know it would have traumatized them, even more, to see me like this.

Chapter 8

THE WORST WAR OF MY LIFE

It was on a Wednesday morning when the psychiatric doctor came in with her two colleagues to let me know that they were moving me to another hospital because they felt it would be a better fit for me. There had been no improvement since I arrived so they felt I would do better in the psychiatric hospital. They told me that there was a bed open which was rare and that the floor I would go to specialized in depression and anxiety disorders. I would need to pack up my things and go that day.

I didn't know what to think, as the thought of going somewhere else, especially to a hospital that was filled with psychiatric patients, made me feel uneasy. I was actually comfortable where I was and felt safe because I knew the other patients and the routine on the floor. However, all I cared about was getting better, so I concluded that this might be a good move for me. Maybe they would be able to adjust the medications and get me well enough to go home quickly. My emotions were all over the place. I felt the horrible hopelessness getting stronger as I now realized my plan of getting on a new medicine and going home in a few weeks wasn't going to happen. It wasn't that simple, and for whatever reason, these doctors couldn't help me at this time.

The fear and terror of never getting better hung over me more than ever. What if nothing worked? What if I ended up being a patient for months? Years? What if there would be no end to this and I would never get to go home again? What if my kids ended up traumatized for life because of me? The questions made my head spin every minute of the day. It felt too much to bear, but I had no choice and needed to somehow do what they told me to do and trust that someone somewhere could help me feel better.

I managed to pack all my things and then was quickly escorted by a nurse outside to catch a cab. I didn't have any time to say goodbye to anyone which really bothered me because I felt like I had relationships with the other patients and wanted to at least tell them where I was going and say goodbye. Even though I had only known them for three weeks, I got quite attached and actually felt grief over leaving them.

The grief together with the depression caused me to cry constantly and uncontrollably for days. I think I cried for a week straight after this day. Another issue weighing heavily on my mind was that my husband and I had planned a trip months before to the Dominican Republic for January of the next year. We had never been to the Caribbean or away for a week together by ourselves and the thought of this not happening only caused me more grief, guilt, and despair. I felt I was letting him down yet there was nothing I could do about it.

It was early afternoon when I arrived at Providence Care Psychiatric Hospital in Kingston. The hospital was about a five-minute drive so we were there quite quickly. I don't remember the nurse ever talking to me on the ride over which was so odd but I soon found out that relying on the nurses for any kind of comfort or encouragement was unrealistic.

I had no idea what to expect at this hospital and could have definitely used some reassurance, but that didn't happen too often. I don't remember being checked in at the new hospital, the nurse that came with me leaving, or anyone talking to me at all, but I sure do remember the sick feeling I had as I walked down the hall of Ward 14 where I was to now take up residence.

As a person who has an appreciation for nice home décor, the first thing I noticed was the discolored and dull walls. Because the building was over 100 years old, there was paint peeling off the walls, any décor was completely outdated, and the atmosphere was cold, lifeless, and institutional to put it mildly. I had never felt so horrified and alone in my whole life! Just when I thought it couldn't get any worse, I was shown my bed. It was surrounded by five other beds with only curtains in between. The walls again had no color, there was no décor except for one old-fashioned and outdated small wardrobe to put our clothes and valuables in.

I don't know how I ended up on a chair in the hall soon after, but I did. I sat there shaking and crying uncontrollably not knowing how I was going to survive. It's not that nice pictures on the walls or a clean smell would have cured me, but it may have at least helped me to feel more comfortable or given me some hope. It didn't help that none of the nurses came over to talk to me either even though their station across the hall from where I was sitting was literally about six feet away.

I still can't believe that another human could ignore someone in this condition and not bat an eye. I understand that a nurse could get quite used to seeing broken people, but refraining from offering any help at all, in my opinion, is completely unacceptable!

As I sat there, another patient actually came over to comfort me which blessed me immensely. I'm sure there were very caring nurses that worked in the hospital at the time but I personally didn't feel very cared for in most of my interactions with them. However, I was thankful to receive some encouragement from the social worker which was helpful.

After I got myself together, I went to my room to unpack my things. As I was putting things in place, a nurse had come in with some papers for me to read. I sat down on the bed to scan over them. I still remember the bolts of fear that went through my body as I read them. The first paper was informing me about electric shock therapy and letting me know that this was one of my options being at the hospital. The other paper was informing me of something called TEMS, a milder form of shock therapy. With electric shock therapy, the patient is put under anesthesia while electric impulses are passed through the brain, intentionally triggering a brief seizure. ECT seems to cause changes in brain chemistry that can quickly reverse symptoms of certain mental health conditions. It is often used as a last resort as many patients wake up with memory problems that can go on for weeks. With TEMS, the patient is awake while it is being performed so it is not as invasive.

I couldn't believe my life had come to this and the thought of undergoing any of these procedures terrified me. It was no comfort either that when you first walked into the entrance of this hospital, there was a historical display set up for all to see which included photos of patients from years ago being tied down and electrocuted. There were many disturbing photos along with some old tools that were used. It looked like something out of a museum or a horror movie, and to the regular person, it may have been interesting, but to me as a patient, it was awful.

Little did I know at the time that I would be spending the next two months on this floor.

There was a mixture of people with different personalities on the floor but we all had been diagnosed with an anxiety or depressive disorder. Some of the patients never seemed to talk to anyone and others didn't stop talking. Some slept most of the time and others wandered around for hours.

On my first night, I ended up in a deep conversation with one of my roommates named Caroline. She heard me crying and out of the mercy of her heart asked if I needed to talk. I found my way over to the edge of her bed and sat down. After some small talk, we started to discuss what led up to us being hospitalized and talked about things we had gone through in the past. We seemed to have quite a bit in common, including our ability to laugh and cry at the same time! The one thing that stood out to me was how we had both suffered extra amounts of grief and shame because well-meaning people had given us advice that had made us feel responsible for our illness. We had both been told by faith-filled people that we could have prayed more or believed more for a miracle.

I want to make extremely clear at this point that there were also many faith-filled people who were gracious, full of love and compassion, with no judgment. Unfortunately the negative can far outweigh the positive, especially when we are vulnerable. The fact is that faith-filled or not, it can be very difficult to know what to say to help someone who is struggling with a mood disorder. I feel that the best thing is to just love the person, encourage them to get the proper medical or emotional help if needed, make a meal, watch their children, and tell them over and over again that they will get better! If they are open to prayer, definitely pray, but never belittle them by making them feel that they can control these illnesses, because they can't. Tell them that this is only a season, and with the proper help, they will get better again.

I feel it was God's grace on me that night to put me in a room with another woman around my age with a similar personality and background. I think Caroline and I both felt a little bit of healing that night just talking through things!

Life on the ward became quite boring as there was nothing to do but get well. How boring is that! There was one lady who came in once a week to do crafts with us or some kind of goal setting, but that was about it. Thank goodness there is now a new psychiatric hospital in Kingston with all kinds of activities for patients to engage in if they have the strength or feel well enough. The new hospital is also completely updated with beautiful decor and new paint amongst other things which makes it a wonderful hospital to heal and recover in!

Every day we would have to be at breakfast at 7:00 a.m., then wait until we were called in to see our doctor. The first time I met mine, it was difficult because he didn't talk a lot and I felt I had no choice but to trust him with my life. I had been told he was one of the best psychiatrists in the hospital, but it was still hard to trust, especially when things hadn't gone well with the medications in the past. Because I had no choice but to trust him, I decided I would.

The doctor wanted to keep me on the medications I was

on for a few weeks to see if there would be any improvements. During this time, I spent my days talking to other patients, going for the odd walk when I had the energy, and trying to believe that I would get better. Something else continued to happen and it still amazes me to this day. People I knew continued to come to see me! I actually had a day planner that I would book my visits in as they were quite frequent and I valued them so much that I didn't want to overlap any of them. These incredible family members and friends would come and sit with me, bring me snacks, make me go for walks and one even brought in a mattress topper and new sheet set. To say I was blessed was an understatement.

The staff began to take notice along with the other patients. Again I had to witness the lack of visitors most people had. It was and still is devastating to me. I can still hear the words of one patient as she turned to me and said, "Lyn, can I be you for one day so I can have a visitor?" It's not that the visitors came to see me because I was so great. I think that because I had never been in this type of hospital before, it was new and fresh to them and because I had been quite the socialite in the past, I had made many connections with people. What I came to understand was that because a lot of the patients had been in and out of the hospital a number of times, or were in for a long time, friends began to drift away along with family members. I can understand how this could happen, but I also understand that the feeling of being abandoned and forgotten would be devastating. Everyone needs other people to show they care, and if there was ever a place that could benefit from volunteers, I would say a psychiatric hospital is a place in desperate need. I will forever be grateful to each and every person who came to see me while I battled the worst war of my life.

Chapter 9

HOPE AGAIN!

I wanted to believe that this was just a season, but all I seemed to see were the patients that didn't leave the hospital for months and even years roaming the halls engulfed by their mental illness. There were people on the floor who paced frantically back and forth full of anxiety, others wailing in their bedrooms, and others who just laid in their beds wanting to die. When you add to that the awful atmosphere of the building, as well as the lack of positive stimuli, you can see why getting well would be next to impossible to believe in.

I actually started to become immune to it all, or at least I thought I was. I think my body just went numb to try and protect itself. One of my roommates was taken out one day on a stretcher because she was completely suicidal. I assumed they were taking her to the other hospital to be put on the "suicidal watch" floor. I remember thinking it was sad, but it didn't bother me like it normally would as it seemed to be one of those everyday occurrences on the floor.

One thing I never got immune to though, was the choking that happened often to one of the patients. Tabitha was one of my favorite patients as she was extremely funny and always ticked off at something or somebody. For some reason, it would make me laugh when I would hear her complain. It's amazing how you can be in the biggest pit of despair and still somehow laugh even though it feels mechanical. I think it was the sound of her voice mixed in with her words that struck my funny bone. Looking back, I am so thankful that there were people like this on the floor who could give me something else to focus on besides my own miserable hell.

One day I was sitting across from Tabitha eating lunch when I noticed that her face turned completely dark red and she couldn't get her breath. I had no idea that this was quite normal for her, so in a panic, I frantically ran to the nurses to tell them that this girl was choking. They didn't seem too concerned and slowly came over to pound her on the back a few times.

She ended up throwing up and then was fine.

On another occasion, as Tabitha was on the phone with her mom I had walked past with a bag of chocolates. She saw them and asked if she could please have one. I asked her a number of times if she was allowed to eat them and she kept saying yes. She promised me she would be super careful and not choke, so I finally gave her one. Not long after, I turned around to once again see her face bright red and her breath gone while still being on the phone with her mom! I was terrified, thinking she was dying and began yelling at the nurses to come help. They were across the hall which I was extremely glad about because I knew they would get there quickly. Well, that was not the case! There were four of them sitting there and no one moved. I kept yelling frantically until one finally got up and told me to calm down and to get away from Tabitha because she would throw up on her own soon and be fine. I couldn't believe it! The nurses just stood there watching until finally, she threw up. Meanwhile, I shook like a leaf, hoping I didn't just end her life! I can't imagine what her poor mother was thinking and feeling. Unfortunately, these choking episodes happened quite often for Tabitha as she had had a tracheotomy surgery in the past which damaged her esophagus and her esophagus was now unusually small that unless her food was pureed or exceptionally soft, she could not swallow it without gagging.

For the average person this may not have been a big deal, but for me, it was extremely traumatizing, as I was extremely hypervigilant around anyone not being able to breathe properly due to the many chokings I had witnessed in the past. The first times I ever saw it was when it happened to my siblings while growing up. I still remember the foods that they choked on. One was a pork chop, another a white- powdered donut, and another was a lifesaver candy. I would run and hide as my parents tried to remove the object. I was terrified the victim was going to die, so in the future when I witnessed other cases like these, my body would automatically go into a cold sweat overcome with terror. Before I even got to the hospital, I had witnessed 10 serious choking episodes of family members and friends where the person could not breathe at all until the object was removed. I guess it makes sense why my hypervigilance got to a point where just the sound of someone coughing would trigger a shot of fear through my entire body. I am happy to say that I have experienced a lot of healing from this in the last few years, and my reactions are not as extreme anymore!

As for Tabitha in the hospital, I struggled a lot because my body was already under immense stress and I couldn't cope well with more, yet there always seemed to be a lot of small traumas like this taking place which didn't help my healing process but only extended it.

After about two weeks of not seeing any improvement in my mental state, the psychiatrist decided to take me off one of the main medicines I was on and switch me to another. I was extremely nervous about this, as I always worried about possible side effects when trying a new medicine. After being on many different medicines throughout the years, however, I have found that the side effects are usually not too serious but more annoying than anything.

I knew I had no choice, so once again I had to trust the doctor. This time he was going to put me on a medicine that treated more than one type of chemical in the brain. It would target serotonin and dopamine. Many antidepressants, along with the ones I had always taken in the past, had only targeted the serotonin levels. I was still on a medication to help me sleep, another antidepressant used as a booster, an anxiety medicine that I could take when needed, and now I was to add this new one. Thankfully, my body seemed to tolerate the new medicine quite well with no major side effects which was wonderful. Time went by and within about three weeks, I started to finally feel a change. The horrific black cloud began to lift, my mind began to slow down a little, and I felt a tiny ounce of hope for the first time in months! The idea that I could get better actually became a small reality again. It was like a tiny ray from the sun had found a small hole to shine through those dark, heavy clouds. It felt incredible!

From this point on, I continued to improve, and after nearly three months of hospital stay, in January of 2013, I was discharged. I became an outpatient which meant that I would still see my doctor on an ongoing basis but didn't have to live at the hospital anymore. I can't accurately express on paper how thankful I was to finally go home believing that I was finally getting well. Hope began to emerge once again!

As I signed the papers to leave the hospital I was informed that I would be on a high priority list for the services of a psychotherapist through the hospital to help me with any emotional support I would need after transitioning back into my home. The only drawback was that the list was long and it would take nine months before I would get that call to say that someone was available. Unfortunately, this was the only support I was offered after being discharged, and I didn't realize how difficult it was going to be trying to go back to a normal life outside of the hospital.

It was probably only after a week of being home when I realized that I definitely needed some help trying to adjust. Even though I felt a little better in my mood, I also felt that I had just been through the war. I was having terrible nightmares about being extremely sick again and having to be put back in the hospital. These dreams would plague me night after night and I would wake up feeling like I was living the past over and over again. The dreams were so real that when I woke up, I would have to remind and convince myself that I really was getting better and not worse.

It was like I was in a daze trying to do the normal routine of life, cleaning my house, making meals and lunches, and yet feeling completely drained from it all. Then I came up with what I thought was a great idea- I decided that it might be good for me to start volunteering at the hospital so I could focus on someone else and help take my mind off of myself.

Soon after I went to the hospital and had a meeting with the volunteer co-coordinator. She gave me different volunteer options and gave me her card when I left. I planned to contact her when I figured out what I could work into my schedule.

In the meantime, my heart was very heavy for the people who were still in the hospital, especially my friend Caroline. I promised her I would come and see her regularly and so I did start to do that. Unfortunately, after I would come home, the memories would start to torment me. Then the nightmares would happen on these nights. I didn't quite understand the recovery process from an ordeal like this at all! I not only had to recover from a serious depressive episode but also had experienced great trauma through it all. There was also grief in that I had lost time with my family and the guilt that I had traumatized them for life because they did not fully understand what was going on. It all felt like too much to deal with on my own so I decided to look for a psychologist on my own as I knew I needed help trying to deal with all these new feelings on top of the old ones. I found someone by looking online and made an appointment. When I first met her I should've known that we probably weren't a good match, but because of the state I was in, I was willing to try anything. In our first session, she told me that I did not need medication, that it was completely useless and was just a Band-Aid. It was not the best thing to say to me at the time as I felt that the medication was saving my life and couldn't even comprehend the thought of not taking it after everything I'd been through. These comments bothered me but I still went back week after week hoping that I would come away with a nugget of hope somewhere and feel encouraged. After about four sessions with her, I had actually felt worse and realized that this person was not a good fit for me.

It is so important for a person to sense a good connection when meeting with someone like a psychologist or counselor. You should be walking away feeling encouraged, hopeful, and looking forward to the next meeting, not worse than when you went in. I knew in my heart that this lady was not right for me, but was concerned too much about hurting her feelings that I kept going back which was so foolish.

I knew I had to find someone else but had no lead on where to go. Then I had a friend give me the name of someone who she had seen in the past and had a good experience with. I contacted this lady, and learned, to my surprise, that she had a daughter who was a social worker and counselor and often worked with people with anxiety and major depression. She recommended I go to her, as she felt her daughter was more specialized in the area. I decided to give her a call and we set up our first appointment.

Chapter 10

HELP TO THE RESCUE

I knew right away at my first appointment with Sandra Bradley that she was the perfect person for me to talk to. As I shared my story with her, she had tears in her eyes and I remember asking her if she was okay! I could not believe her compassion and empathy. At the end of our first session, she gave me a hug and my response was, "Wow, I'm not used to this kind of treatment." She replied with, "Lyn, sometimes I just can't help it." I was so moved when I left because I felt strongly that God was watching out for me and that He had led me to Sandra. Sandra was amazing at listening to me, encouraging me, and teaching me, and after every session, I would leave full of hope. It was the perfect fit!

In our first session, Sandra had asked me about my childhood, which was interesting to me, because although I didn't quite understand how this was going to help me with my current situation, I trusted Sandra's approach. As I explained my childhood years, Sandra seemed to think that it totally made sense why I would be struggling so much emotionally and be dealing with a chemical imbalance. She explained to me how we are all created with needs, the need to be nurtured, loved, appreciated, encouraged and listened to. I know my parents tried their best, but with seven children, it was impossible to meet all of their children's needs, so some of mine had gone unmet. When the traumas occurred, I didn't think to talk to them, as I did not want to add more stress to their lives as I knew they were busy. I also had no idea that the traumatic situations were affecting me beyond a day after they took place, as I was somehow able to push them aside and move on.

Sandra then began to explain the effects of trauma on a person and how they can impact our lives, especially in childhood.

Through Sandra's teaching and my own research, I have discovered that when trauma takes place, especially in a young child, it can affect the development of the brain in an extremely negative way. Because the brain is still developing until a person is in their early twenties, the wiring can be changed by trauma so that the child can actually be more prone to more of it down the road if it is not dealt with properly. Children don't naturally have the skills to process extreme trauma, and if they aren't sharing it with others, which is often the case, they don't heal from it but rather develop unhealthy coping mechanisms. They often do not have the words to express how they have been traumatized or feel safe enough to share it with anyone. This can lead to many different issues such as behavioral problems, emotional numbness, anxiety, disassociation, feelings of shame, anger, intense fear, and sleep issues.

My unhealthiest coping mechanism was shoving down all emotions that I felt were negative, like anger, sadness, grief, and fear. I learned from Sandra that there are no negative emotions, that they are never right or wrong, but that they just are. It is what we do with them that can cause problems if they are not handled correctly. I certainly did not manage them correctly, as I totally disassociated from them, which was not healthy, even though it had made sense to me to do so at the time.

I decided to share my new revelation with a few close friends who were part of the team I was still on at the church at the time. One of them felt strongly that it would be a good idea for me to write out any experiences that I considered traumatic in childhood. As I wrote out my list, she asked me to tell her about them. All the experiences were from about age four until about age fifteen. There were approximately fifteen situations that I had remembered clearly and that had caused great ongoing fear in my life. Some of the situations on my list included a dog attack I experienced when I was four, the choking incidents, a car accident I had witnessed where body parts were laying in pieces on the sidewalk, visiting my dying relatives, the deaths of close relatives, being present while my siblings experienced severe injuries on several occasions, being in a few car accidents myself, being in a tornado, and getting caught in rocks under the water and nearly drowning to name a few, and several others on my list that I prefer not to share publicly.

The traumas continued right through adulthood. One that stood out happened in my first year of marriage. My husband and I had gone to Niagara Falls for a weekend to relax shortly after my recovery from my first bout of depression. We were walking down the main road on a nice sunny day when a man came flying out of a bar behind us, beating another man over the head with a pool cue. The man was full of blood and could barely walk but was trying to run. Everyone on the street started screaming and running for cover. It felt like we were in a movie. I didn't know where Jeff had gone, but I ran into a store to hide behind a clothing rack, terrified. It turned out that the man was from the Mafia, and according to reports, that his drug deal had gone wrong. Interestingly, as I shared all these incidents with my friend, my voice was completely monotone with no emotion except for laughter at times, as the list sounded so ridiculous after awhile. My friend asked me if I felt anything at all about them and I said, "No". I very clearly learned that day what the meaning of emotional numbing and disassociation was. It was obvious that I had totally shut down my emotions concerning these events because I had no notion of how to process them. No wonder I had extreme anxiety as I got older!

It never made sense to me that I didn't have depression or anxiety issues that I could remember when I was young, but as an adult, I was being hit with it hard without any obvious cause in my mind. It's like all those feelings of fear, horror, and terror were undercover for years and the stress of my present-day circumstances were forcing them to emerge with a vengeance. It was all making sense to me. My brain was not wired to be able to cope with so many traumas, and as each one came, my body's coping skills were getting weaker and weaker until finally there were none left.

I would never say that trauma is the root cause of all depression and anxiety, but I certainly believe it can play a huge role. When I was in the hospital, I noticed that early traumatic experiences had happened to many of the patients I had talked to. The effects of shock and trauma can never be underestimated as they definitely affect us in more ways than we know at times.

This realization became even more clear to me as Sandra and I began to talk through my experiences in the hospital. Since being home I found that I was still feeling very weak and vulnerable after a month and it really bothered me. In my mind, I expected to feel a lot more like myself but instead was battling a whole new set of emotions even though my depression had begun to lift.

Sandra began to explain to me that trauma is caused when a person feels trapped and fearful at the same time. If a person experiences something frightening but has control over the situation and can remove themselves, they will be less traumatized. Trauma affects everyone differently but when a person has no control over the events, they will automatically be more traumatized.

I had now experienced more shock and trauma since being diagnosed with depression and anxiety which clarified why I was feeling so fragile after being out of the hospital. In the previous year, I had no control over my emotions, whether the medication would work or not, what doctor I would get, what I would witness in the hospital, or when I would get out of the hospital. Sandra told me that she believed I had Post Traumatic Stress Disorder because of the symptoms I was experiencing as well, especially the flashbacks, unpredictable emotions, and hypervigilance which is the fear of the trama happening again. I was never formally diagnosed with PTSD by a doctor, but one thing was sure, I was once again extremely traumatized.

When I realized that I was not only dealing with healing from a chemical imbalance but also symptoms of more trauma, I was able to accept the unpredictable journey a little better. Just having an explanation for what I was going through was so helpful and critical to my recovery journey. In the bible, there is a verse that says "Then you will know the truth, and the truth will set you free." It is one of my favorite verses now as I have seen first hand how when the truth is brought into a situation, freedom can come. This is certainly what it felt like for me!

I was beyond grateful to have found such a wonderful counselor and have close friends that were able to support and help me walk through my journey of recovery. Good support is so vital to anyone who has experienced trauma of any kind and help is needed to walk through and past it. As difficult as it can be, it needs to be talked about in order to move forward so a person can become a victor and no longer a victim. This is exactly what I wanted- to move beyond the past and not be controlled by it for the rest of my life!

Chapter 11

THE ROCKY ROAD TO RECOVERY

The journey of recovery wasn't easy for me; there were many ups and downs but it did eventually happen. Before it did, however, I was still finding it difficult to go back into the hospital to visit patients or attend appointments. Sometimes I seemed fine when I was there but when I returned home, all of the memories would hit me again. I would have horrible flashbacks and nightmares for days and it really irritated me. My thinking was that if I just kept going back and facing my fear, it would go away. As they say, there is a time for everything, and this was definitely not the time to be facing my fear and putting that extra stress on my body and mind.

I had booked an appointment with Sandra to share with her my desire to volunteer at the hospital in an effort to focus on something other than my own issues. She looked at me very lovingly and said, "Lyn, that's a very nice thing to do but just so you know, your recovery will take at least a year. Your brain needs that amount of time to heal along with your body. Going back into a place that reminds you day and night of your illness is not a good idea. Maybe after a year or two, you can look at volunteering." My jaw must have dropped because I couldn't believe it was going to take that long to heal. In the past, it seemed to take only a few months, but I would learn that with every new depressive episode, the length of recovery time lengthens and no two episodes are ever the same.

Six months after I was discharged I experienced an unusually bad day and was not coping well at all. Since it had taken every ounce of my being to deal with treating the depression for so many months, my body was in a state of shock and numb to emotions like the grief and trauma which accompanied my treatment experience. In a previous appointment with Sandra, she had explained to me how there are stages of recovery from trauma, which are very similar to grief. There can be shock, anger, and deep sadness, which is different from depression. On this particular morning, I was having a really hard time being alone, was crying again, and didn't know what to do. I was experiencing so many different emotions at once and it was overwhelming to me. Particularly difficult was that the grief I was experiencing felt just like depression and I couldn't tell them apart. I started to panic thinking my medication wasn't working anymore. I have since heard that it is quite common for people who are recovering from a serious episode of depression to second guess their medications' effectiveness. Any emotion that feels similar to depression can trigger complete panic and an overflow of negative memories or a fear that they are moving backward in their recovery.

This was certainly the case for me and I would battle this thinking for many months because recovery is not a smooth ride. First, there are a lot of bad days with a few good days in between but after time, the good days outnumber the bad ones until wellness comes and the chemical balance is restored.

As time went on and I had fewer bad days, I began to trust that I was truly recovering so I didn't react as strongly to having a bad day. It took a lot of support for me to feel this way and many times I would ask people if it was normal for me to feel sad or down in certain situations. It was so easy to assume I was not well again. Friends would need to tell me many times that, yes, it was completely normal, and that assurance would be enough to relieve me of any anxiety. Once fully recovered, I found myself needing to ask that question to people less and less.

However, on this one particular day when I was struggling, I decided to call my friend, Bonnie, to tell her what was going on. I was so grateful she sensed that I needed someone with me and offered to come over because I didn't want to ask. When she arrived, I was a mess, as the fear that I was going backward was heavy on me, along with a huge dose of hopelessness.

I can't stress enough the importance of talking to someone when we are struggling with something that we can't handle alone. Sometimes, it is the most difficult thing to reach out and admit to someone else that we need them. It can make us feel weak and vulnerable. It can be extremely humbling. Yet I have learned that it is vital for our health in every way. If we can find even one person that we know will love us unconditionally no matter what we say or how we look, reaching out can change our day, our week, and even our lives for the better. It was Bonnie I called that day because she had been an extremely safe person for me to confide in. No matter the situation, she never ran away or shut me out, but loved me unconditionally. I am so blessed to still have her in my life!

Soon after Bonnie arrived, I began to share with her what I was struggling with then we ended up having a cry fest together. What I'm going to tell you next is truly a miracle in my opinion. Bonnie and I both believe in the power of prayer. She decided to pray for me that day. Before she did, however, she felt that it would be good for me to talk to God out loud and tell him exactly what I was feeling and why. Even though I felt extremely safe with her, it still wasn't easy for me to express these things in front of her but I felt that it was the right thing to do. I made a list of all the experiences that had caused me grief and trauma in the last year. Then I sat there and I talked to God like He was sitting right on my sofa with us. I told Him I was angry He would allow this to happen to my family. I told Him I was terrified that it would happen again. I told Him I felt completely abandoned by Him throughout it all and didn't understand what I had done wrong to deserve it. I was very specific about any situation that I could think of and told Him exactly what I felt about it with great emotion. To be honest, it felt amazing to speak it out. In the past, I would have felt that I was being irreverent or disrespectful or rude to God, but for some reason, this time I felt He loved me unconditionally and could handle anything I said because it wasn't a surprise to Him. He knew it all anyway.

After I was done rattling off my thoughts to God, Bonnie said a simple prayer and it drastically changed my day and my future. She asked God to come and remove all the effects of the trauma off of me. I know something miraculous happened after that prayer because I never again had another nightmare concerning the hospital after that day. I truly began to recover and heal in my body, soul, and spirit. Something happened inside of me where I felt a peace that I hadn't felt in months and I knew there was nowhere else it came from except God himself. This is why I now believe so strongly that it is extremely important to address the spirit, soul, and body together for complete healing.

In the past, when I would go visit Caroline in the hospital, I would have constant triggers, but after that day, when I visited her, the triggers disappeared. This doesn't mean that all the memories disappeared but the terror, fear, and sadness associated with the memories began to melt away.

Recovery was still rocky. There were days when I felt I was moving forward and days when I was sure I was headed back to the hospital. During my emotional journey, I ran into another unexpected hurdle that I needed to cross. As grateful as I was for the support I was receiving through Sandra and my close friends, I couldn't help but be hurt by the lack of support given to me by others who had known me well for years and knew my situation. They didn't reach out to me when they knew I was hospitalized or when I was released. When they did see me, they didn't mention anything to me about what I was going through. It seemed to me that they would actually try to avoid me. This really upset me because I knew that if I had been in a car accident, I would have been treated entirely differently. People would have seen the injury and asked how I was feeling. Unfortunately, because they could not see the inside of my mind, they had no idea of the horrific pain I was going through and many were probably afraid to ask because it would have been difficult to know what to say. This is completely understandable in awkward situations but like a person grieving the loss of a loved one, I needed to be asked how I was doing. I didn't have nurses and doctors doing it anymore on a daily basis. I think people felt that because I was out of the hospital, I was all better and the past was behind me. When in reality, the hard work had just begun. More than ever I needed people to show me that they cared and that I wasn't alone on the journey. A simple hug or the words 'how are you feeling?' would have been more than sufficient.

I also still needed to hear that my mental health was improving, as it was hard to believe it at times and every day was a battle. My body was physically weak and my mind still felt fragile. It felt like a vase that had been completely shattered and finding the right medication put a few pieces back together. Every encouraging word was like taking a piece of that broken glass and connecting it with another. One by one the pieces would be put back together but it would take time.

I felt selfish and ungrateful that I was even allowing these thoughts to bother me as I had so many others who were supporting me, but Sandra reminded me that feelings are never right or wrong and they are all valid. They needed to be brought into the light and worked through in order for me to move forward. Suppressing or denying my feelings would only do more damage than good, making room for possible anger and bitterness. This would only add more fuel to the fire and not aid in the healing process at all. That was the last thing I needed, so even though it took time, I chose to forgive those who I felt hurt by and move on. As I healed more and more, I could think clearer and realized that no one was intentionally trying to worsen my condition but they honestly did not know what to say or they didn't realize I was still so broken.

As I continued to recover, Sandra shared with me a beautiful visual of what recovery looks like and it helped me immensely to feel hope for the future. In one of our sessions, she got out a paper and pen and drew a person with a big circle around them. I was the person and the circle represented the depression and anxiety. It was around me because it was huge and all-consuming, affecting every part of my life. Then Sandra drew another picture where the person representing me was larger and the circle was small and off to the side. This illustrated what recovery looked like. Depression and anxiety would someday only be a tiny piece of my world and my life would revolve around others again. I would regain my true identity. This hit me so deeply because it's exactly what I was experiencing. Before I was sick, I took great pride in the fact that I was a hard worker, a fun, loving mom, a wife, as well as wearing many other 'hats'. As I became ill, I felt like I lost my identity completely and forgot who I once was. I have never forgotten those drawings, as they speak so clearly as to how anyone can feel when they have any type of illness. It can be easy to believe that the illness will always be a huge part of your life and that you will never be able to focus on anything else. But I can tell you from experience that this is not true! You can get better; you can recover, and you can think about other things beyond what you are struggling with today. If not today, then down the road!

As the medications did their work and I received more and more revelation through Sandra, joy, and health eventually made their way back into my life. My mind started to calm down and hope returned. It was a tough battle because, in the beginning, relief would only last a few hours. There were times when I was convinced I wasn't well again and started to panic. When it felt unbearable, I would call my close friends or Sandra. They were all so good at just listening. I knew it was extremely difficult for them to have to listen and not be able to fix me, but thank goodness they did because it helped me immensely. Sandra and Jeff always told me repeatedly that I was going to get better, which is exactly what I needed to hear. I should have written it down on a piece of paper, hung it on my wall, and repeated it every day because it was very difficult for me to see the good changes in myself. I often felt like there weren't any positive changes, which made me feel defeated and hopeless again very quickly. This is why hearing it from Sandra and Jeff was so vital to my recovery. Even if I didn't believe it all the time, I would try and trust them enough to tell myself it was true. Self-talk is so powerful.

During my recovery, I knew I had to be vigilant in putting things in place for self-care. No one was going to do it for me, especially no one from the hospital as the only person I was still seeing there was my psychiatrist. This led me to try attending a few support groups. One was a group specifically for people dealing with depression and anxiety and another one was for anyone struggling with any type of mental illness. I tried to go a few times but found that I would come home feeling worse than before I went. This was a good indicator that it was not a good group for me to keep attending. After a number of meetings, I found it too difficult because many of the people shared depressing stories that didn't offer me any hope but actually made me entertain the idea of being dysfunctional forever. For some people, these groups may be helpful if they are making progress in the group and hope is offered, otherwise, I would suggest avoiding them.

Besides seeing Sandra on a regular basis, I also asked Bonnie if we could meet once a week just to have a visit as I knew I didn't have to pretend with her and could just be myself no matter how I felt on any given day. She graciously agreed to this and we kept up meeting like this for about two years as we really enjoyed our times together. I was also able to contact my friend Kim whenever I needed too, which brought me great comfort. These wonderful friends were such a gift to me!

There were other things I did to help myself which I will share with you in a later chapter. They can not only speed up recovery but prevent having to deal with depression and anxiety in the first place.

Chapter 12

NEW REVELATION

After about a year, I felt that I was finally moving on. I gained back the weight I had lost; I felt joy again on most days, enjoyed being at home, and started to get involved again with things I couldn't do the year before. When I left the hospital, I was on high doses of two different antidepressant medications along with a sleeping pill and an anti-anxiety medication I could take as needed. My goal was not to wean off all the medications. I was told I would be at a ninety percent risk of relapse and there was no way I was risking that. However, after some time, I was definitely interested in weaning off some of the medications because I wasn't sure if I still needed them all.

It was necessary to have my liver checked on a regular basis. One of my medications was very toxic to the liver, so I knew continuing to take it would not be a good idea long term. I decided it was okay to wean off the sleep medication a few months after being home because my sleep returned to normal and I was thrilled to have one less medication to pay for and take.

I noticed that as the antidepressants started to really do their job and I did my part in the recovery, I was not needing to take the anti-anxiety prescription anymore either. This left me with high doses of two medications. I was content with that until about two years after my discharge from the hospital. My doctor agreed with me that I could begin to wean off one of the medications, which is exactly what I did with no problems. Weaning off can be very difficult so it is incredibly important that a doctor is involved in the process. I have heard stories of people doing it themselves only to run into all kinds of trouble.

I am happy to say that I have been on a low dose of one antidepressant since 2015 and have never felt healthier. I believe there are a number of reasons for this. During my weaning process, I began to really dig into looking at ways to stay healthy so I would never have to go through this again. For the first time, I saw the value in addressing many things in order to heal and not just rely on the medications to cure me. I asked God many times during my recovery process to direct me, to open and close doors, to educate me, and to connect me with the right people in order to find my healing. I feel like He did this for me even though my recovery didn't happen the way I expected it to or in the timeline I had in mind. My patience had never been tested to this degree in my life and I hope it never will be again even though I see the benefits to it now and see the worth in all of it!

I have had to make some major changes in my life that I had never made before because I didn't know about them or had not believed those changes could make a difference. Everyone has a different journey to health and wellness. As I've mentioned before, there is no one thing that will cure everyone, especially when it comes to mental illness. This is why it is so important to address recovery and prevention according to a persons' individual mental health needs. It is very important that everyone finds their own healing and never assumes that what worked for someone else will work for them. On the other hand, what may not have worked for someone else could work wonders for you.

I imagine that we all have a "mental health and wellness" tool belt. There are different tools that can be put in our belts. Some may have many tools and others may not depending on their life experiences but the more helpful tools we have, the better our chances for healing and prevention of mental health struggles are. The tools will be different for each individual which is very important to realize. It is never helpful to compare ourselves to someone else and think that we can just do what someone else is doing to feel well. I have had many people ask me how certain medications have worked for me when they have had to start one. I always tell them that they can't compare to me because they need to see for themselves as the same medicine can work very differently for each person. Doses will be different along with side effects and tolerance. We are all so unique and different which is a very good thing even though it would be nice to just have a simple solution to our struggles and do what someone else has done to relieve them.

One tool that was not helpful for me while recovering was the Internet. I was driven to look up every medication online and read peoples' comments on them hoping that it would encourage me, but that did not happen at all. The Internet is full of negative comments on how medications don't work and of all the horrible side effects people suffer. There must have been some encouraging stories somewhere, but for whatever reason, none of the ones I found were helpful. Looking up information online was a very poor idea for me and I would not recommend anyone else doing this, as it can cause more stress, which in turn, slows down the healing process. It would be better to have someone else search for, and find, the positive and hopeful comments or stories and print them out for you to read or send your way.

I personally could not handle any negative stories during my recovery. I needed to hear and read about other peoples' success stories. I needed to fill my mind with accounts of people who had overcome depression and anxiety, who went from dysfunctional to functional. I am sure this is the case for anyone suffering from any kind of illness. It is not helpful to hear about all the people who die of cancer every year if you are diagnosed with it. It is much better to focus on the people who conquered it and lived to tell the story.

The most important thing I learned through my healing process was that I had to address issues in every area of my being- body, soul, and spirit- in order to have the healing I have today. This doesn't mean that I will never struggle again, although that is my hope, but I feel that I have better tools now to prevent another severe episode from occurring or to work through any struggles that arise in the future.

As we know, depression and anxiety can vary in severity but there are basics to recovery which everyone can benefit from knowing to aid their effort in maintaining emotional and mental health. I will share some of the tools I have gained with you in the hope that they will be helpful to anyone reading this. Healing did not come easy for me and it took a lot of work and support but I cannot even begin to describe to you how undeniably worth every effort it was.

Chapter 13

ADDRESSING THE BODY

Nutrition and Diet

Medication definitely plays an important role in treating mood disorders, but it is only one piece of the pie so to speak.

Years ago I was told that by one of the psychiatrists. At the time, I wasn't ready to hear it and didn't want to believe it. I wanted to believe that medicine was all I needed to stay well. However, my thoughts have changed dramatically since then. After my hospital stay I began to ask myself, if a medication was all people required to stay well, why were so many people continually switching their prescriptions so often? And why did mine stop working? These questions caused me to look for answers.

Most of us have heard the saying, 'you are what you eat,' which can sound a little harsh but I believe it is very true. Eating right doesn't guarantee that you will never get sick or develop depression or feel anxious but it will definitely lower the risk. Sometimes it can be overwhelming to try and put all kinds of things in place to prevent sickness, and for each person, it is important to figure out what you can realistically implement. I am just sharing what I have personally learned, and try to implement in my own life so that my risk of experiencing depression and severe anxiety will be significantly decreased.

The goal with our diets is, not only to consume nutrient-rich foods, but also to help our body be in a state where these nutrients are received. It doesn't do much good if we eat all kinds of nutrient-rich food but our body is so toxic that it cannot absorb the nutrients.

We live in a day and age where toxicity seems to be everywhere. The food we consume has changed dramatically from decades ago, now containing added preservatives, antibiotics, hormones, sometimes it is genetically modified and much of it is processed. Then add in the polluted air we breathe, the chemicals added to our water supply, chemical-based home cleaning products, lack of exercise, and lack of sleep. It is no wonder most of us are extremely toxic in our bodies and unhealthy. I came across a quote a few years ago, which spoke volumes to me. It goes like this: "We were never designed for the sedentary, indoor, socially isolated, fast-food laden, sleep deprived, frenzied pace of modern life." Historically, people did not live as we do now and when it comes to brain disorders, statistics show that they were rare, unlike today. This tells us something!

In the last few years, I have been drawn to research the body and understand better ways of preventing disease, especially mood disorders. The good news is that there is a lot we can do to treat and prevent them. We don't need to live in fear of everything around us, but knowing and understanding the times we are living in is extremely helpful and beneficial for us. Knowledge gives us the power to make better choices.

The body is such an amazing gift and if given the right environment, can often stay well or heal itself from illness. This is the way God created it, but it can be quite difficult in this day and age, with all the toxins and chemicals working against us. Often our bodies are either not receiving enough of the right nutrients or not able to absorb them properly. Doctors can be very helpful with prescribing the correct medication but I have found that it is just as important to see someone who is specifically trained in nutrition to uncover the root causes of disease. Looking at the root is vital to not only getting well but staying well.

Out of all the research I've done in the past few years, what has influenced me the most has been the fact that the digestive system itself is a rich source of neurotransmitters, which carry signals inside the brain and body. In fact, and to my surprise, ninety-five percent of the neurotransmitter serotonin and half the dopamine in the body are produced in the gut! I had always assumed the neurotransmitters were made in the brain. Not only this, but I had the idea that the antidepressants I took increased the number of neurotransmitters in my brain, which is actually not the case. The medications can only work with the neurotransmitters we have in our body, so if we don't have many, the medications won't work very well. This revelation has given me loads of hope as I have often felt very helpless in the past to control when I would be hit with the next depressive episode. We are not helpless and this is great news!

Consuming probiotics is one way that we can help ourselves, as our gut needs the right amount of good bacteria in order to produce enough neurotransmitters to keep us mentally healthy. Our gut contains both good and bad bacteria and they need to remain in balance. Often the bad bacteria far outweighs the good because of our diet, pollution, chemicals in prescribed pharmaceuticals and over the counter drugs, and other factors which lead to many health problems, including imbalances in brain chemicals.

Probiotics are good bacteria that our gut needs in order to work well. Taking probiotics is a very simple thing to do and yet can provide enormous benefit by helping our bodies provide the neurotransmitters needed for our brain to remain healthy. Probiotics come in capsule form; but another less expensive way is to get them through eating fermented foods like sourdough bread, sauerkraut, kombucha, and kefir.

Fermentation involves a process where microorganisms, such as bacteria or yeast, are used and converted into carbohydrates to alcohol or organic acids under anaerobic conditions. This process is what creates good bacteria known as probiotics.

One thing to remember however is that unless you buy these products in a reputable health food store, many will carry dead probiotics because of the way they were processed and packaged, or because of a long shelf life.

I was thrilled to learn how to make my own kefir this past year and it is very simple! It involves having a few 'kefir grains', which you can purchase at a health food store or online, mixed in a jar with 2% or whole milk. The neat thing is that people who are sensitive to lactose can often handle kefir because of the fermentation process. This mixture is left on the counter with a coffee filter and elastic band around the top of the jar for about two to three days until it ferments and becomes a yogurt-like substance. Then it goes in the refrigerator and is ready to consume. It's that simple! The kefir grains can be used over and over again. The drink can be put into a smoothie if the taste is too bitter. I will admit, it is not like drinking chocolate milk but it is easy to get used to.

Our diet plays a critical role in mental health and no medication will ever make up for a bad diet. What we eat and drink directly influences the structure of the brain, which in turn affects the way the brain functions. In the past few years, I have been grateful to be able to volunteer at the psychiatric hospital doing patient visits, which I enjoyed immensely. However, I couldn't help but notice what the patients were eating and drinking- soda after soda, coffee, chocolate bars, chips etc. Those are not the type of food or drinks needed to help a person get well.

Caffeine has been proven to work directly against many medications and often patients will take their medications with their coffee. I did it too for years because I didn't know that it wasn't a good idea, but when I found out, I cut it out and mostly drink only decaf. Caffeine also exasperates anxiety so it is one of the worst drinks to have when struggling with a mood disorder. Decaffeinated coffee and herbal teas are a much better choice.

Another thing I have come to understand lately is the importance of eating organic. In the past, I didn't pay attention to this, but with all the chemicals sprayed on our foods, I feel like it almost does more damage than good to eat them sometimes. Yes, organic is more expensive but if we eat less but eat well, we even out our spending to include organic foods.

I love having a garden, especially when it flourishes, so we can eat fresh produce throughout the summer and then freeze more for the winter. It is definitely extra work to keep it up, but it gives me an opportunity for exercise and allows me to save money on groceries.

I recognize that growing a garden is not enjoyable for everyone and that the idea of eating organic can be overwhelming and seem impossible. Ideally, it would be great if organic was all we ate but realistically, for many people, it probably won't be. I love what is called the 80/20 rule where the goal is to eat at least 80% nourishing foods and allow for 20% of things which are not as healthy. I feel that if we put expectations on ourselves that are completely unrealistic, we set ourselves up for failure, which can be frustrating and cause us to quit trying. I'm all about balance! A chocolate bar or greasy burger once in a while won't kill us, but if most of what we consume is dead, lifeless food then we really can't expect to be well.

Ison M. Haas, MD, an author and expert on health and nutrition, states in his book, Staying Healthy with Nutrition, that individual foods, as well as various types of diets, contribute to our wellness and that both natural food nutrients as well as chemicals in the form of synthetic contaminants and food additives affect brain function and neurotransmitter levels. He points out that food reactions, allergies, and hypersensitivities also affect energy levels, moods, and mental faculties as many people experience milk and dairy product-related reactivity because of an inability to digest lactose, which is the main ingredient in cow's milk. Wheat, which contains gluten, is another very common reactive food that should be limited in the diet and replaced with other grains like amaranth, quinoa, tapioca, or rice. Other common food allergens include corn, soy products, and peanuts. Sugar, especially refined sugar, and sweet foods like soda and candy, foods refined with white flours and rice, although not considered allergens, alter the glycemic index and are associated with rapid mood changes and depression.

In order to protect brain health, Dr. Haas recommends getting all the appropriate nutrients from wholesome foods and supplements, avoiding chemicals and junk food as much as possible. Finding out which foods may be causing allergic reactions or sensitivities in order to avoid them is also important. Eliminate, limit or completely remove sugar and refined foods from the diet, minimize the use of caffeine and alcohol, eat an abundance of fresh vegetables, fruits, nuts, seeds, whole grains, and legumes. He suggests taking supplements as well as eating a healthy diet, which can help prevent mood disorders because of the many vitamins, minerals, and amino acids that support brain function, specifically serotonin levels. They also support normal hormone balance, especially of the thyroid and adrenal glands.

The following is a list of the vitamin and mineral supplements as well as herbs, which Dr. Haas suggests helps the body ward off depression.

- B6 (pyridoxine) assists brain function and neurotransmitter functions. Use along with a general B vitamin complex, 50 to 100mg twice daily after meals
- B12 along with Folic Acid supports nerve structure and functions
- Vitamin C and Pantothenic Acid aid the adrenal glands and energy
- Choline and Inositol aid the brain
- Calcium and Magnesium allow relaxation and better sleep when taken at night
- Iodine supports normal thyroid function
- Zinc and Magnesium, as well as the L-Amino acids can improve energy
- Primrose Oil and Flaxseed Oil increase prostaglandin E1 production
- Good quality multivitamin/mineral
- St. John's Wort (but not if on antidepressant medication

as they interact)

- Valerian and Hops for insomnia
- Kava Kava for anxiety
- Ginseng for energy
- Siberian Ginseng for stress

Please Note: Consult with your practitioner before starting to take any supplements listed here as they can do harm rather than good in certain conditions, as some should not be taken at all if pregnant or breastfeeding. The information I provide is for your own research purposes only.

Another supplement that is extremely important for mental health is omega 3 fatty oils. bebrainfit.com states that the omega 3 essential fatty acids, in particular, are one of the most beneficial groups of nutrients for your brain and overall health. There are two main omega 3 fatty acids- EPA (eicosapentaenoic acid) and DHA (docosahexaenoic acid). DHA is unarguably the most important omega 3 for brain health, accounting for 97% of the omega 3 fatty acids found in the brain.

Here are some interesting facts from bebrainfit.com:

- Deficiency of omega oils is widespread- it's estimated that 70% of Americans have insufficient levels of omega 3
- Low levels of omega 3 have been linked to anxiety, depression, and bipolar disorder
- Medical students facing pre-exam stress exhibited a 20% reduction in anxiety when taking omega 3 supplements
- A review of studies in people with mood disorders found that omega 3s have significant antidepressant properties

- After only three weeks of supplementation, an impressive 67% of study participants no longer met the criteria for being depressed
- Omega 3s have been found to be helpful for major depressive disorder
- Eight weeks of EPA supplementation was shown to be as effective as the popular prescription antidepressant fluoxetine for treating major depressive disorder
- When EPA was taken along with fluoxetine (the antidepressant Prozac) the results were significantly better than either fluoxetine or EPA alone

This is one supplement I am very strict about taking for obvious reasons! But again, consult with your practitioner before starting on any supplements.

Taking supplements can feel overwhelming and become quite expensive so it is important to figure out what works well for the individual. If on antidepressant medication, it is also very important to ask a pharmacist or doctor if there are any interactions with natural products, especially herbs.

Exercise

Exercise has been proven to be as effective as antidepressants in some people. It raises serotonin and dopamine levels. Anyone will benefit from exercise, but those of us who are short on neurotransmitters could certainly benefit from exercise. It not only raises neurotransmitter levels but also helps us detox amongst many other health benefits.

I try and get my exercise by doing things I actually enjoy, like fast walking. I know I will likely stick to that on a regular basis. I've learned from experience that running every morning or going to the gym five days a week isn't realistic for me. Fast walking is, I can listen to music or even watch videos while on my treadmill. Finding exercise that you enjoy and that makes you feel good will highly increase your chances of staying consistent with it. The options are endless, from walking and swimming to going to a gym. According to experts, the goal should be to have a significant increase in heart rate for a minimum of twenty to thirty minutes four days a week in order to experience the mental health benefits.

Restful Sleep

Sleep is more important for us than we realize sometimes. I used to compare myself to others and be upset if I couldn't feel rested after six hours of sleep. Well, the reality is that I need about eight to nine hours a night to make it through the next day without napping. Sometimes, even more, especially before and during 'that time of the month' us women experience. I have children that are often up until after eleven at night and I'm up early to help pack lunches and make sure everyone has eaten breakfast in the morning before they leave for the day. I need my sleep! Of course, I don't always get enough but in those times, I try and make sure I nap when possible. I know sleep deprivation can be a trigger for mood issues.

I don't rely on caffeine to keep me going so a proper diet and sleep is really important to me. I decided to switch to decaffeinated coffee four years ago and it has honestly changed my life in that I don't feel like there's a jackhammer inside of me after consuming coffee. My blood sugars stay level; I am more relaxed, and I don't experience the crash when the caffeine wears off. I feel so much more stable, energetic, and rested, as my sleep isn't affected with insomnia resulting from the caffeine. I also feel good knowing that the caffeine is not working directly against my medication.

A note on coffee: I do drink a good organic decaf and enjoy it just as much as caffeinated coffee. However, I try to only drink decaf which has had the caffeine removed through the Swiss Water Process and not with chemicals, again something to consider when switching to decaf. Although it was difficult to switch from caffeinated to decaffeinated coffee at first, after some time, I didn't even notice the difference.

If the goal is lasting recovery from mood disorders, big changes may have to be made. I can tell you from experience that they make a huge difference! I know this because I have been through more stress in the last few years since my healing and recovery than I have in my entire life and I did not end up sick with depression, which would have been the case in the past!

Chapter 14

SOUL & SPIRIT HEALTH

When I speak about the soul, I am referring to the mind, will and emotions of a person. It helps for the brain to be treated first on a physical level especially if there is a serious chemical imbalance in the brain before the soul of a person can be addressed. Trying to address the soul while the brain is still sick often proves to be a vain effort. The soul can be damaged for many reasons and in order to heal from the damage, professional help is often necessary.

Even though counseling or psychotherapy was recommended to me in the past, I never looked into it until after my hospital stay. Besides the fact that I didn't think I had a need for it, I also felt like it was a huge sign of weakness and something that would embarrass me. That belief system was quickly abolished when I went to my first few sessions with Sandra and realized my great need for counseling along with the strength I received leaving a session. Professional counseling played such a critical role in my recovery and still does today, helping me to stay well. I continue to go back to my counselor if I am struggling with things that I find difficult to talk about with friends or family or that I don't want to burden them with. It is a place where I don't have to worry about anyone else but myself. I don't have to worry about hurting anyone's feelings or watching their reactions. I don't have to protect anyone, which gives me great freedom to express my emotions freely and get them out. Going to a professional for help is far from weak and can actually be a sign of great strength and humility.

If we can allow someone else to speak into our lives and help us get to the root of why we are struggling, it can often bring healing that we would never have attained on our own. Even though family and friends can offer a lot of help, a professional who is outside our circle of family and friends can often give us an entirely different perspective, and sometimes a more accurate one as they are not as emotionally involved.

There are many things I have learned so far about myself through counseling that have been extremely helpful to me. As I have mentioned earlier, one of the main issues I have struggled with most of my life has been the tendency to feel too much responsibility for others, often causing me to become a 'rescuer'. A rescuer feels like they need to help everyone else fix their problems, and in the meantime, often forget about their own. They thrive on taking on other peoples' responsibilities, which often leads to them being enablers and co-dependant. This is exactly what had happened to me and especially manifested in my own family and with the people I cared about deeply. Numerous times I went overboard trying to 'rescue' my husband and children or friends by taking on responsibilities that should have been theirs to carry. In the meantime, my needs went unmet and self-care wasn't even in my thinking. Before jumping in to help someone else, it is extremely helpful for me to ask myself a few critical questions. Do I have a responsibility in this? What is my responsibility in this? What is the other person's responsibility?

For example, if someone is struggling with an addiction, it would be my responsibility to love the person and encourage them to get the professional help they need but it is their responsibility to actually go to the professional and receive the help. If I step in and set up their appointments and drag them there after trying to convince them that they need help, it will most likely be a waste of time.

There is a saying I have found extremely eye opening that states, 'we teach people how to treat us'. If we teach others that we will always be there to save them or take on their responsibilities, they will continue to depend on us and never learn to be responsible for their own lives. We will be co-dependent enablers that get worn out, dragged down, and eventually become resentful and miserable. This can definitely contribute to a lack of mental health.

As I continued to do some deep soul searching on my recovery journey, I also realized that I was one of the worst 'people pleasers' I knew. For whatever reason, it had always mattered to me what people thought about me. I have never liked the idea of someone being upset with me or not liking me, which has caused a lot of extra stress in my life. I have read that people who are determined not to hurt others find the pit of depression much more frequently than people who are aggressively hurtful. This makes complete sense to me because emotions are often buried by 'people pleasers'. They fear expressing them and risk having someone react. I still find this area difficult but am learning how to let people know when I am upset and why. I still cringe when I do it and try to be as gentle as possible, but it is incredible what happens to my insides and the relief it brings when I am honest, even if people aren't happy about me sharing. I have learned that their reaction is not my responsibility. My responsibility is to keep myself healthy in every way possible and expressing emotions in a proper way brings about health.

Holding onto certain emotions can also cause sickness. Experiencing emotions is not wrong but a part of normal life. However, some emotions can definitely become unhealthy if they are not worked through properly or quickly. There are many reasons as to why people carry around unhealthy emotions. It can happen very easily and I think we all struggle with this at one time or another. Working through, and staying free, from these emotions can be very difficult and yet, it is so important for mental health. If we are consistently carrying toxic emotions around, such as bitterness, resentment, offence or ongoing anger, we can expect both our physical and mental health to be compromised.

I have found that forgiveness is a huge key to staying free from many toxic emotions. It is far from easy at times and may have to be repeated daily, or sometimes even more frequently than that, but it is so necessary in keeping ourselves mentally well. There is a quote that sums up quite well what unforgiveness can do to us. It says that, "Unforgiveness is like drinking poison and expecting the other person to die." I feel this is a very accurate analogy as the other person is totally oblivious to how we are feeling but we are the ones carrying around all the extra stress and toxicity, harming ourselves in the process. This stress and toxicity can lead to many issues, such as relational problems and a variety of different illnesses in the body.

Feeling emotions, like anger, short term is not unhealthy in itself but it can become unhealthy if we choose to stay in it. There can be huge consequences to our mental health. It is much more beneficial to see a friend or counselor if we need to and work through the pain that has caused us to be in that place so we can find freedom.

In the medical world, there is something called CBT, which stands for Cognitive Behavioural Therapy. It basically involves challenging our thought patterns when we are feeling strong, unpleasant emotions such as fear, sadness, discouragement... etc. When a negative thought comes into the mind, the idea is to write the thought down along with the unpleasant emotion associated with it. The goal is to change the emotion by changing the thought. The challenge is to write down an alternative thought, one that is more positive, which in turn, helps to change the emotion to a more pleasant one.

I talked earlier in the book about how a social worker in KGH taught me about CBT. Even though I felt the timing was not good for me, the technique can be very useful when the brain is not severely depressed because changing our thinking can definitely change our mood.

The Spirit

I see the spirit as the part of us that houses our conscience, identity and creativity. Our spirit plays a very important role in how we act and think, not only about ourselves but about others too. If we feel something is off or unsafe about a person or situation, we often refer to it as a 'gut feeling'. That gut feeling or instinct can be seen as our conscience. Many times when a person has great damage in their spirit, especially their sense of identity, they will have a hard time discerning what is right, wrong, safe or unsafe. I'm sure we have all experienced situations where we have seen others do something so obviously wrong and thought, 'did you not think before you did that?' or 'how dumb could you be?'. Often, because of severe damage in their spirit, their conscience has been beaten down and the 'gut feeling' is no longer there, resulting in bad decision making.

There are many reasons for damage in a persons' spirit. Trauma of any kind, especially in childhood can be a major cause for great damage in a person's spirit and affect how a person copes with life. Betrayal, a dysfunctional family, bullying, and abuse are only a few examples of why there would be damage. These are very difficult things to work through but the good news is there can be healing from them. Many people with mental health issues are able to find great healing when they include spiritual help in their lives.

Someone in spiritual authority can be very helpful to a person in these circumstances, especially if they have training in counseling. I have had the privilege of sitting with someone like this and it has definitely affected me in a positive way, bringing more health to my life than I ever expected.

For me, as a Christian, I feel I can connect with God. When I am feeling stressed, anxious, or alone, I often talk to God about it or in other words, I pray to Him. It is a great release, causing me to feel much more peaceful. Everyone needs to figure out their own way of gaining peace spiritually but it has been scientifically proven that prayer affects the brain in a positive way. Brain specialist, Dr. Caroline Leaf, states that,

It has been found that twelve minutes a day of focused prayer over an eight week period can change the brain to such an extent that it can be measured on a brain scan. This type of prayer seems to increase activity in brain areas associated with social interaction, compassion, and sensitivity to others. It also increases frontal lobe activity as focus and intentionality increase. As well as changing the brain, another study implies that intentional prayer can even change physical matter. It has been proven that toxic thought can cause brain damage but prayer can reverse that damage and cause the brain and body to thrive. How truly amazing!

This naturally leads me into talking about the importance of good community in our lives. I don't think anyone was created to go through this life alone and we all need a sense of family or community. We need a place where we can feel loved and accepted unconditionally. If we are not able to receive this through our biological families, it is important to receive it elsewhere. This is why I enjoy going to church- not only do I have a community of people there who love and accept me for who I am, but I also get to receive the gift of prayer at times.

One day, while I was volunteering at the hospital doing visitations, I started to talk to a patient who seemed to be in and out of the hospital every few months. We first talked about her medications but then she mentioned to me how, when she went home, she went home to only a cat. She had no family and I don't recall her talking about any friends or being involved in anything in her community. After she shared this with me, it made perfect sense why she would sink back into the blues so quickly. How depressing! She actually told me that the hospital was like her family and she didn't want to go home. When a person actually feels more community in a psychiatric hospital than in their own home, it is extremely sad. Yet, this is how many people live. This demonstrates how important it is to connect with people and build relationships to experience the blessing of community.

I think the amount of community a person needs will vary depending on a person's personality, but everyone needs some sense of community. Being an extrovert, I have noticed that if I am not around enough people in a week, my mood can start to shift to where I feel down. I personally need a lot of interaction with others in my life in order to feel good emotionally. My son, on the other hand, is more content to only have his family as his community, along with his online gaming friends. Even though everyone is different, a sense of community is extremely important for all of us, whether we know it or not.

A good community can encourage our sense of identity- what and how we feel about ourselves. We need people to speak positively into our lives in order to become confident in who we were created to be. It's important to choose the right kind of community in order for this to happen. If we surround ourselves with negative, draining people then it will be very difficult, if not impossible, to feel good about ourselves, let alone feel happy. It is also important that we learn to speak positive words over ourselves as well.

There have been numerous studies done on the power of words and how they can change the atmosphere. There was an experiment conducted with water that amazes me. It was done by Dr. Masaru Emoto in 1994. In his experiment, he collected water from different parts of the world and put them into petri dishes. He labelled some as 'good' water and some as 'bad' water. For weeks, he spoke words of love, encouragement, and gratitude to the 'good' water and also played positive and peaceful music over it. In the same way, he spoke hate and distaste to the 'bad' water, along with playing heavy metal music to it. Then he froze the water and examined it with microscopic photography.

The results were astounding! The water that received positive words had formed into beautiful crystal formations and the water that received the negative words looked distorted, destroyed and ugly.

Dr. Emotos' experiment proved that our words have a direct effect on the physical world and that they actually affect the molecular structure of water. This is extremely powerful when we think of how we are made up of over 70% water! We can impact the health of our bodies with what we speak over ourselves and are definitely affected by what others speak over us! I have seen similar experiments online done with plants and rice and the results are the same! This is why it is so important to think about how we speak to ourselves and others!

Another area that I find extremely important to care for in my life is the area of creativity. I believe that all of us have creative power but it may demonstrate itself in different ways. What has fascinated me is the correlation there seems to be between creativity and the mental health of a person. I have found that if there are areas in a persons' soul or spirit that have been extremely damaged, they will often find it very hard to be creative. For example, I had a friend who always said she wasn't creative and actually hated creativity but once she began to receive counseling into some of her deep issues, she began to operate creatively and loved it. It was amazing to watch!

Therefore, in an effort to find healing and freedom from mental health challenges, we cannot neglect our soul and spirit. Complete health will only occur when we address our body, soul and spirit together.

Chapter 15

DETOXIFICATION

I believe detoxification is a major key to our health. It is extremely important to detoxify in every area of our life, such as our body, relationships and with anything that causes us to feel stress consistently. Then we can enjoy optimal health, especially mental health.

The Body

Often we don't realize how much stress is put on the body when we are living with toxic overload but it is huge. Picture the parts of a car as our organs. Over time, the parts become clogged and dirty, the car begins to break down and needs a tune up. This is exactly what happens to our bodies. They can only take so much stress and toxicity before they start to break down. I believe that the body was created to cleanse itself of toxins. However, in this day and age, with all the extra chemicals, pollutants, additives and toxins, our bodies need a little help.

It doesn't need to cost a lot or be difficult. I have found

that there are many different ways to detoxify our bodies. As our liver is the main detoxing organ, it can be very beneficial to cleanse it at times, especially when taking medications for any reason, as they do contain harmful chemicals despite the relief and help they offer.

I decided to purchase one a few years ago online through a company called Global Health. I didn't know what to expect but the results were amazing! The whole process was fascinating to me. Through following a strict six day long diet and drinking a liver cleansing formula and apple cider vinegar drink, I was able to remove many gall and liver stones and lost close to seven pounds because of it.

Detoxification is an amazing way to lose weight! I did not even know there was such a thing as liver stones, but apparently, most of us have them just from living in this day and age. For me, the cleanse was incredible and I would recommend it to anyone. There are many liver cleansing kits available, but it is important to make sure that the diet is adjusted appropriately for the days when using the kit to get the best results.

Not only is it important to detox the liver, but every organ of the body. General wellbeing and mental health is negatively affected by toxic buildup. Toxins are stored in the intestines, gallbladder, kidneys, liver, lymph system, fat cells, and skin. When there is an overload of toxins that the body's own detox system cannot keep up with, the colon becomes sluggish and the liver gets congested and unable to filter blood effectively, kidneys weaken in their attempt to get rid of excessive toxins that collect in fat cells, tissue, and between cells. All this results in a reabsorption of toxins into the body. By this point, the body becomes fatigued, mood swings can be filled with fear, anxiety, nervousness, and a lack of mental clarity occur. Sleep is negatively affected, and sickness and depression move in.

Juicing vegetables or making smoothies and fasting also helps to rid the body of toxins and give the body a rest from processing so it has time to rebuild, repair, and strengthen itself. Juices build nutritional reserves and detox the body because they are rich in antioxidants that bind to toxins and carry them out of the body. Drinking extra filtered or purified water to keep the body hydrated helps flush waste through the system as well.

A simple way to detox the body on a regular basis is by drinking one cup of warm water in the morning with half a squeezed lemon in it before eating or drinking anything else. Lemons cleanse, purify, rejuvenate, and detoxify, especially the liver, as they help in fat metabolism.

It is important to choose alkaline foods over those that produce acid in the body as an overly acidic body is toxic, encouraging bacteria, viruses, fungus, and yeast to thrive. Food that becomes alkaline in the body nourishes, strengthens, and gives the body energy. Lemons contribute to alkalizing the body because they turn alkaline when ingested, even though they are acidic outside the body. Apple cider vinegar is very similar.

The skin is the largest organ and sweating is one of the best ways to detox because it moves toxins out of the skin. Once this happens, it is a good idea to use a loofah or skin brush to remove the toxins from the skin. In countries like Europe, saunas are a normal part of life and are used regularly as a method of detoxing and improving health and wellness.

Again, there are many different ways to detoxify the body and it is well worth the efforts!

Relationships

Relationships can bring us the most joy in life and also the most pain. They can be healthy and uplifting but also sick and toxic.

Relationships that bring stress and negativity into our lives should be limited. This can be very difficult, especially for people who tend to be 'caregivers' or 'rescuers'. It can be so easy to get in over our heads with other people and develop dysfunctional relationships without even realizing it, all in the name of trying to help. Many things can make a relationship toxic, from co-dependancy to abuse. Or it can be a friendship where one person is controlling and manipulative while the other plays the victim. If we allow these kinds of relationships in our lives, they will be very detrimental to our mental health. We all need relationships that are positive and enjoyable, where we feel 'filled up' and not completely stressed out and drained. A healthy relationship is two sided, where we receive as much as we give.

It is nearly impossible to avoid all stressful relationships but if we have good boundaries and enough healthy relationships, we will be better equipped to handle those relationships which strain us.

Stress

There are many things in life that cause stress and we can't always avoid them. Although, we can limit stress and choose how we deal with it.

What exactly is stress? Stress can be defined as a "physical, chemical or emotional factor that causes bodily or mental tension." Stress can come from our external environment, our thoughts and our body. Financial hardships, relationship issues, negative thinking, and toxicity in the body are all examples of what can cause stress in our lives.

When we feel stress, there is a 'fight or flight' response where the body will release stress hormones to allow a burst of strength and endurance. The heart speeds up, muscles tense, digestion stops and blood flow to the brain and muscles increase up to 400%. After repeated instances of this, the reaction can bring harm to your physical, mental and emotional health. Research shows that chronic stress can lead to mood disorders such as depression and anxiety, amongst other disorders, so it is critical to limit stress as much as possible.

For stress that we can't control, it is extremely important that we cope with it in a healthy manner so that we are not throwing more 'fuel on the fire'. Smoking, drugs, drinking alcohol and overeating are examples of unhealthy coping mechanisms. These things will only increase stress levels and do nothing to help us.

For myself, I have found that exercise helps me to feel calmer or speaking with someone. Often, just talking to a friend about what is bothering me is enough to lift some of the stress off of me.

Taking vitamin B is an excellent idea for anyone dealing with high amounts of stress because this vitamin often gets depleted by our bodies' response to stress. B vitamins can help us by working with brain chemistry and balancing neurotransmitters, thus aiding us in achieving balance over stress.

Meditation is also an excellent idea for relieving stress. I meditate by thinking about verses in the Bible that mean a lot to me and then I talk to God about what's bothering me and ask Him to take my stress. When I do this, I sometimes picture me lifting my hands full of my concerns up to Him and dumping them in His hands so that I don't have to carry them anymore. Meditation is a very personal thing but the end result should bring a sensation of peace and well being inside of ourselves.

Chapter 16

FINAL THOUGHTS

Some symptoms resembling depression can be similar to normal emotions, but when they are uncontrollable, severe, and last for long lengths of time, it is definitely wise to make a doctor's visit.

The following is an overview of what I have learned about mental health disorders through my own research and knowledge gained in trying to understand my condition and its severity, as well as in seeking out help from those qualified in the field. I am sharing my findings here to encourage those of you who are struggling with some of the symptoms I will cover here, and to aid you in deciding whether to seek out professional help or not.

To help understand and be able to distinguish whether or not a person may need medical intervention, let's take a look at the differences between discouragement, situational depression, dysthymia, major depression, seasonal depression, postpartum depression, and manic depression, also known as bipolar disorder.

Discouragement

Discouragement is an emotion that can manifest many emotional symptoms but it is transient, with an obvious cause, and the person affected is still able to enjoy other aspects of their life. It can resolve in time with good support and a discouraged person can continue to be hopeful and have good thought control. Discouraged people feel relief from the comfort of others, unlike a person who is severely depressed.

Situational Depression

Situational depression is usually brought on by a stressful event, such as the death of a loved one or a health issue like an illness or injury. Sometimes people require medication for a season until the event has resolved; but if the depression is milder, counseling and a good support system along with proper self-care can be sufficient, allowing the individual to cope until the stressful situation subsides.

Dysthymia (also known as Persistent Depressive Disorder-PDD)

Dysthymia is a milder form of depression that is just as treatable as depression, often requiring the same medications. From what I've learned, many people who struggle with this may not even know they have it because they are so used to living with it. However, once they receive treatment, they are amazed at how good they feel and realize how much they were suffering.

Dysthymia is characterized by a depressed mood for most of the time continuing for at least two years with at least two of the following symptoms accompanying it:

- Poor appetite or over eating
- Insomnia or oversleeping
- Low energy, always tired
- Low self-esteem
- Poor concentration and difficult making decisions
- Feeling hopeless

Dr. Grant Mullen (Emotionally Free, page 79)

Major Depression

From my own experience and research, I have learned that major depression is the most severe form of depression, as well as depression resulting from bi-polar disorder. It definitely requires medication as it is completely debilitating and puts a person at serious risk of suicide if left untreated. It is a result of a chemical imbalance in the brain and cannot be changed by just talking about it. Self-care is almost impossible to do because the symptoms are too severe.

Major depression doesn't always have an obvious trigger and can come on quite suddenly, however, a situational depression can trigger a severe enough biological reaction that it can turn into major depression.

Bi-Polar Disorder (also known as Manic Depression)
A person with Bi-Polar disorder requires medication. From what I've seen, it usually takes more than one medication to treat this type of depression.

Bi-Polar Disorder is characterized by wide mood fluctuations cycling between deep sadness and despair to extreme happiness, euphoria and mania. These cycles can vary in length. Some cycles are referred to as rapid cycling where the mood swings fluctuate very quickly back and forth and other cycles can last for months.

Lack of sleep can trigger a manic phase and then continuing lack of sleep will fuel and intensify a manic episode.

Seasonal Depression

Seasonal depression is a less severe form of depression but can be quite disruptive. It often causes a person to feel unmotivated, 'flat' or 'down'. It is usually present during the winter months in areas of the world where it is very cold and there is a lack of sunlight. Some studies have shown that over 80% of people who live in cold climates are vitamin D deficient due to the lack of sunlight which gives us vitamin D. This vitamin is extremely important for the brain and mood control. It is definitely worth checking into your vitamin D levels if you are struggling with seasonal depression. If levels are low, often a supplement is all that is needed to correct this.

Postpartum Depression

Postpartum depression may start during pregnancy or at any time up to a year after giving birth. For me, it happened four weeks after I gave birth to my daughter. Not to be confused with the 'baby blues', postpartum depression symptoms are much more severe and debilitating, lasting much longer than a few days. Medication is required to bring the chemicals in the brain back into proper order.

The following is a list of symptoms for depression and anxiety disorders, which I discovered in the book, *Emotionally Free* by Dr. Grant Mullen. (page 77-80)

Depression:

- Persistent sad, anxious, or empty mood most of the time most days
- Feelings of hopelessness, pessimism, and low self-esteem
- Feelings of guilt, worthlessness, helplessness
- Loss of interest or pleasure in hobbies and activities that were once enjoyed, including sex
- Insomnia, early-morning awakening or oversleeping
- Loss of appetite and/or weight loss or over eating and weight gain
- Decreased energy, fatigue, feeling 'slowed down' or agitation that can't be controlled
- Procrastination since simple tasks seem harder
- Thoughts of death or suicide, suicide attempts, constant feelings of 'Life isn't worth living like this'
- Restlessness, irritability, bad temper, never relaxed or content
- Difficulty concentrating, remembering and making decisions due to persistent, uncontrollable cluttering of down, sad, negative thoughts that can't be kept out of the mind

Other common symptoms of depression include:

- Persistent physical symptoms that do not respond to treatment, such as headaches, digestive disorders, and chronic pain
- Continuous anxiety that can't be turned off, uncontrollable worry about small things, including physical

health

- Social isolation or withdrawal due to increasing difficulty making small talk
- Other relatives with depression, alcoholism, or nervous breakdowns
- In children, increased irritability, persisting complaints of physical problems, agitation and unwarranted anxiety or panic, social withdrawal

Mania

- Exaggerated elation and rapid, unpredictable mood changes
- Irritability, impatience with others who can't keep up with you
- Inability to sleep, not needing sleep, too busy to sleep and not being tired the next day
- Big plans, inflating self-esteem, exaggerated self importance, impulse of overspending
- Increased talking, louder and faster and can't stop
- Racing and jumbled thoughts, changing topics rapidly, no one can keep up
- Poor concentration, distractibility
- Increased sexual desire, uninhibited, acting out of character or promiscuous
- Markedly increased energy, 'can't be stopped', erotic, aggressive driving
- Poor judgement, no insight, refusing treatment, blaming others
- Inappropriate high risk social behaviour, brash, tell-

ing people off, overreaction to events, misinterpreting events, distortion of meaning of ordinary remarks
- Last hours to days, usually ending with a crash into profound depression

Anxiety
- Restless, keyed up, or on edge
- Tired frequently
- Difficulty concentrating or mind going blank
- Irritability
- Muscle tension
- Difficulty falling or staying asleep

Panic Attacks (also a characteristic of anxiety):
- Sudden fear/terror takes over
- Tingly sensation
- Profuse sweating
- Difficulty breathing

When it comes to recovery and helping someone to heal from depression and anxiety, I believe that timing is everything. A good first step for anyone struggling in this area is to make an appointment with the family doctor. If the doctor feels that medication is required, he/she may recommend one or give a referral to a psychiatrist, someone who specializes in brain disorders.

Medication can bring a person to the surface when they feel like they are drowning and will enable a person to put other things in place to aid in the healing process. It is next to impossible to attend counseling sessions or change a diet when a person can barely function or think.

As I mentioned earlier, when I was first admitted to the hospital in my depressive episode, I was asked to go to CBT (Cognitive Behavioral Therapy) sessions to learn how to change my thinking. Needless to say, this type of process was quite senseless to me at the time. With my brain functioning improperly and not being able to control any of my negative thoughts, trying to replace them with positive thinking was not going to happen. Dr. Grant Mullen speaks about how our brain can be compared to a house with doors and windows. When our brain is working properly and we have good thought control, we are able to close the doors and windows to reject any thought we don't want. However, when we have a chemical imbalance in the brain, this is not possible. It is like all the windows and doors are open and every single thought that comes our way is allowed to move right on in. In depression, the thoughts are always negative which just adds fuel to the fire. Trying to fight them off is exhausting and in my experience, impossible! This is where anti-anxiety medications can be helpful as they work within an hour and help to slow down the mind. I am actually surprised, looking back, that CBT was offered on the floor of the hospital where I was because it was a crisis floor. This meant that most of the people there were extremely sick mentally and not even functional. I believe that CBT is an excellent tool when a person can think straight, and it did help me down the road, but again, timing is everything.

In my darkest moments, what helped me the most were people just demonstrating that they cared. Hugs, and people telling me over and over again that I was going to get well, helped me the most along with talking to people who had 'been there, done that'.

If you know someone struggling with mental illness, it is a good idea to ask him or her what they need and what is helpful, not assuming anything. For example, you might think the person wants you to bring them a coffee every morning when they really don't want it because they are too nauseous or have no desire for it.

If you are someone dealing with a person whom you feel could use help but is not interested, my heart truly goes out to you. It can be such a difficult road when a person won't receive or recognize their need for help. I've been down this road before and I would say that prayer may be your greatest hope of that person getting the help they need along with unconditional love and good boundaries for yourself. It is difficult enough for people who are supporting a person willing to receive help, let alone a person that refuses help.

Self-care is extremely important for you if you are dealing with a loved one who is not receptive to getting help. I have spoken to a number of people who attend counseling sessions for themselves as the caregiver, to aid them in coping with the stress of those situations.

With all the help and knowledge available these days, there is no reason for those with mental health disorders not to pursue healing. It may feel and look impossible, but it is not! It can take time and effort but it's well worth it. Often there is short term pain for long term gain! It is also extremely beneficial to seek out help early on if possible and practice preventative measures so that unnecessary pain and long recovery journeys can be avoided.

In the summer of 2018, I became a single mother to 2 teenagers after a 22-year marriage. It has been the hardest trauma I have ever had to face and everything I have written in this book has been put to the test. I have had to pull out every single tool I've ever collected in my "mental health" tool belt and put them to use. Have there been days where I have cried on and off for hours or felt anxious? Most definitely but I would not be human if I didn't feel these things in this type of situation. I have had sleepless nights, moments of intense anger, times of great sadness from all the loss but am happy to say, there has been no depression, panic attacks or anxiety issues to the point of needing more medication or being put into a hospital! This shows me that the rocky road I have travelled in the past has not been in vain. I have learned so much and there has been progress along with deep healing which I could never have imagined years prior. I now know without a shadow of a doubt that there is truly value in putting effort into self-care to help cope with the stresses of life. All of us will feel ups and downs in our lives and maybe like we are even drowning at times, but if we are willing to seek and accept the help that we need, we can rise again.

There is always HOPE for the HOPELESS!

Acknowledgements

I can't imagine being where I am today without the love and support of so many.

To BONNIE RUTTER: I can't thank God enough for putting you in my life. Your encouragement, visits, prayers, hugs, listening ears, unconditional love and ability to see the good in me when I didn't feel there was any, have impacted my life forever. You are one of the best gifts I have ever received!

To KIM LABRECQUE: You have been there for me through thick and thin. I will be eternally grateful for all your encouraging words, love, and concern in the times I needed it the most. Thank you for listening to me process out loud on the phone for hours when you could have been doing something else. You often spoke the words I needed to hear and gave me the strength to get through those dark days. I appreciate you more than you know.

To all the staff and families at KINGSTON CHRISTIAN SCHOOL: I can't thank you enough for the love you poured out on my children as they walked through an extremely traumatic time when I was hospitalized. Not only did you love my kids but you loved me with your prayers, visits, kind notes, and updates on my kids to help ease my mind when I was in the hospital. What a beautiful community you are!

A special thank you to MICHELLE DICKISON, and GRACE KIRKLAND who came to visit me daily in the hospital for the first month without barely even knowing me, but out of pure compassion. Grace, I will never forget your gift of new bedding and a mattress topper because you were concerned about me getting a good sleep in those hospital beds. Michelle, your snacks, walks, talks and prayers will never be forgotten.

There were many friends that came to not only visit me in the hospital but sent small notes just to ask how I was doing on a regular basis. This meant so much. My sincere apologies for not being able to remember every person who did this, but please know that your acts of kindness did not go unnoticed.

Thank you to JULIA KOOY, ILSE CONTOIS, MARI VEPSALAINEN, RHONDA KOTCHAPAW, PATRICIA BLANCHET, SARA CHAMPAGNE, SARAH GONSKE and BONNIE MUNDY who spent many hours of their time encouraging me, visiting me, watching my children when it was needed, and praying for our family.

KAREN BANDY, you have been like an older sister to me for many years. I am so thankful for that first booklet of Dr. Grant Mullen's that you gave me, your sofa that you let me lay on when I wasn't well, your encouraging words, prayers, and heart to see me well. What a blessing you have been!

Thank you, SHARI DOSEGER for being there for me as I walked through my first episode of depression. I'll never forget the day that I was able to get off your sofa and enjoy your soup after not being able to enjoy food for weeks. What an amazing gift it was!

I feel a deep sense of gratitude towards my counselor,

SANDRA BRADLEY. We have been on quite the journey! You have taught me so much - not only about the roots of my own depression and anxiety but also how to truly be empathetic and sincere when listening to others. Your empathy and compassion were exactly what I needed when I first met you in the condition I was in. Anyone can go to school to be a counselor but not everyone has empathy and compassion like you do. In my books, this can mean the difference between a good counselor and an amazing one. You are an incredibly amazing counselor! The words " thank you" don't seem to be enough for all you have given me.

To my wonderful parents, LUKE and SHIRLEY LISE: thank you dad, for releasing mom to come 4.5 hours to stay with my family until there was some improvement in my health. This eased a great deal of my stress as I constantly thought about how I couldn't be there for Jeff and the kids. And mom, thank you so much for all the work you did on this book - you offered wonderful suggestions, spent time editing and publishing. You are one of the most gifted people I know!

To PAT and DON STAFFORD: thanks to Pat for getting on a plane from Florida and fly all the way here to help take care of your son and grandchildren when we needed the help. And thank you to Don for being supportive of this.

I am so thankful to both sets of our parents for not only helping on the home front but for praying and visiting as well. You are deeply appreciated.

To JEFF: Thank you for your love and support through the years. When I was sick with my depressive episodes, you were amazing at telling me over and over again that I was going to get better. Even though I didn't believe it, you still continued to tell me that I wouldn't be sick forever which is what I needed to desperately hear. It encouraged me and gave me the strength I needed to get through those tough days.

Thank you to the doctors and nurses who work in psychiatric hospitals. You have an incredibly important job and can make a huge difference in the lives of your patients, especially with what you say. I am extremely thankful for the encouraging words I received in both hospitals I stayed in and the efforts that were made to figure out the right medications for me.

Thank you to everyone who believed that my life experiences were worth sharing and encouraged me to write this book. It's been quite a process, but with your encouragement, it has happened.

I love you all!

And last but not least, my heart overflows with thanksgiving to God who I believe is the giver of all good gifts. The Bible says in Romans 8:28 that in all things, God works for the good of those who love him, who have been called according to his purpose. I feel that God has done this for me and can do it for anyone. He is able to bring good out of the worst situations if we let Him,

Blessings, Lyn Stafford

Resources

Orthomolecular Medicine

The approach to psychiatry that incorporates the use of nutrients to rebalance brain chemistry is described as or orthomolecular therapy. Readers can obtain referrals to trained orthomolecular psychiatrists and physicians in the United States and Canada by calling Orthomolecular Health Medicine in San Francisco at 415-922-6462. Many physician members of the American College for the Advancement of Medicine (ACAM) and most naturopathic practitioners also have training in the treatment of depression using nutritional supplements and herbs. ACAM referrals can be obtained by following the instructions at 800-532-3688.

Books:

Mind Over Mood- Change how you feel by changing the way you think- Dennis Greenberger, PhD, Christine A. Padesky, Phd

Emotionally Free- Grant Mullen, M.D.

Who Switched off my Brain?- Caroline Leaf

Juicing, Fasting and Detoxing for Life- Unleash the Power of Fresh Juices and Cleansing Diets- Cherie Calbom MS, CN, with John Calbom, MA

Websites:

bebrainfit.com

Dr. Daniel Amen- http://danielamenmd.com

Dr. Masaru Emoto- https://www.youtube.com/watch?v=au4qx_l8KEU

Global Healing Center- https://www.globalhealingcenter.com

Please feel free to share your thoughts with the author at: lynastafford@gmail.com

Made in the USA
Lexington, KY
03 June 2019